CONTENDING
FOR THE
FAITH

FRED MORITZ

Fred Moritz

Gal. 6:14

God bless you, Jason

Bob Jones University Press
Greenville, South Carolina 29614

Library of Congress Cataloging-in-Publication Data

Moritz, Fred, 1942-
   Contending for the faith / Fred Moritz.
     p. cm.
   Includes bibliographical references and index.
   ISBN 1-57924-361-4
    1. Fundamentalism. 2. Christian life—Biblical teaching. 3. Bible. N.T.
Jude—Criticism, interpretation, etc. I. Title.

BT82.2 .M68 2000
230'.04626—dc21

                                  00-038455

Contending for the Faith
by Fred Moritz

Design by Jenny Shahinian
Composition by Agnieszka Augustyniak and Beata Augustyniak

© 2000 Bob Jones University Press
Greenville, South Carolina 29614

ISBN 1-57924-361-4

15 14 13 12 11 10 9 8 7 6 5 4 3 2 1

To Dr. Frank Bumpus—pastor, soul-winner,
Fundamentalist, separatist, friend, and encourager

His invitation to speak at the 1998
Fundamental Baptist Fellowship meeting prompted
the study that resulted in this book.

Table of Contents

Foreword

The first and foremost fundamental of the Niagara Bible Conference of over a hundred years ago was the inspiration of God's precious Word. It was apparent then, as it should be now, that unless one has a solid infrastructure of truth, it is impossible to build a meaningful superstructure. Thus the Bible was the bedrock upon which Fundamentalism, a new name for age-old Bible Christianity, continued its ageless, meaningful existence. Attacks from the time of German rationalism (modernism so-called for its recent advent) onward have been launched by religionists and atheists alike; but, as the old hymn expresses it, "The Bible Stands."

How amazing then that in the closing days of the twentieth century and, doubtless, the closing days of this dispensation of grace, one should find the very foundation of "the faith" brought into question. A few years ago a popular book titled *The Battle for the Bible* made its appearance, but, to be sure, the battle has grown into all-out warfare. A new front has been opened, and now many who call into question the divine authority for Fundamentalism profess themselves to be Bible believers.

I cannot fully express my delight that in the face of the present confusion, Dr. Fred Moritz, executive director of Baptist World Mission, has accepted the challenge to address the matter. Surely this present work clarifies the present situation, while speaking with authority concerning the divinely inspired, inerrant, infallible, integral Word of God. Have we a God-breathed message to declare to a sin-sick world? The answer, as this work will demonstrate, is a resounding, unequivocal yes.

–Dr. David Cummins

Acknowledgments

"No man is an island," said John Donne. The work on this volume has vividly reminded me again of that truth. I owe a debt of gratitude to many who have aided me in this task. In May of 1998, Dr. David Cummins insisted that I commit this work to writing. He read the entire manuscript as it developed and made many valuable suggestions. Besides all her other work as my secretary, Mrs. Judy Owens proofread the entire manuscript. My daughter Mrs. Christin Dupee provided much needed (and sometimes ruthless!) first-draft editorial work. Dr. Bruce Compton, Dr. Larry Oats, and Dr. Warren Vanhetloo are esteemed theologian friends who provided excellent suggestions for improvement at certain places in the text. Dr. Dan Olinger and the Bob Jones University Press staff worked with the excellence that characterizes all they do. Finally, my wife, Judy, encouraged me in the task and spent many hours alone while this book took shape. My heartfelt thanks goes to each one.

INTRODUCTION

Since 1981, the Lord has given me the privilege of serving at Baptist World Mission. Each year we conduct an orientation seminar for our new appointees and missionaries on deputation. In 1988 Dr. Charles Hatchett, director of Camp Joy in Whitewater, Wisconsin, invited us to hold our annual seminar at that beautiful camp and conference center, located on the shores of Whitewater Lake. We have gratefully enjoyed the kindness Dr. Hatchett and his staff members have shown us each year.

Dr. David Cummins, co-author of *This Day in Baptist History* and now deputation director for Baptist World Mission, leads the annual orientation seminar. As our concentrated, week-long seminar ends, Dr. Cummins gives our missionaries an evaluation sheet. He asks the missionary families who attend the seminar to make suggestions for improving it the next year. We read and evaluate all the suggestions, and we implement many of them in the following year's program.

Stopping for Self-Evaluation

In any worthwhile activity, self-evaluation is beneficial. When a task is begun with certain goals in mind, evaluation helps to ensure that the goals are met. What do we now see that we did not understand when we began? Have we made mistakes we should correct? What can we do better or more efficiently? How can we make this project more useful? Can we save money as we go along? Answers to these questions may point out serious errors, bruise our egos when we see our mistakes, or simply show us the need for minor corrections that could vastly improve the work. In any case, evaluation is helpful.

Fundamentalists also do well to evaluate themselves and their movement. This book will argue that Fundamentalism is

1

really an expression of New Testament Christianity. Fundamentalism as we know it crystallized as a movement in reaction to liberalism. The movement has changed in the hundred years or so since it appeared. Early Fundamentalists opposed the inroads of higher criticism, evolution, and the resulting theological modernism (also called liberalism) when it began to infiltrate their denominations. They fought from within to save their denominations until the battle was hopelessly lost. Either they separated from the apostate organizations or the denominational political leaders expelled them. The next generation of Fundamentalists formed new educational institutions and fellowships of churches. In 1947 New Evangelicalism appeared on the scene. Some leaders with Fundamentalist heritage had come out of the apostate denominations but soon capitulated to New Evangelicalism. They formed association or entered into dialogue with the very apostates whom the first generation of Fundamentalists had opposed.

An Evaluation of Fundamentalism

Where do we stand today? What is the present state of Fundamentalism as a movement? Have we strayed from our original purposes? Are we standing today as firmly as we should? These questions merit consideration. We who unashamedly embrace a biblicist, separatist position and heritage should seriously evaluate ourselves, our ministries, our conduct, and our direction. Liberals and New Evangelicals have examined and analyzed us as thoroughly as my family doctor pokes, pricks, prods, taps on, and listens to me when I have my annual physical! Many are amazed we still exist as a movement. Some of the liberals and New Evangelicals are objective in their evaluation of us, and others border on slander as they write. If others examine our movement, we can only aid our cause by honest self-evaluation. More than forty years ago, Dr. Chester E. Tulga, who served as research secretary for the Fundamental Baptist Fellowship, voiced the same opinion:

> It is our conviction that fundamentalism as a movement can best be understood by those who were a part of it, who participated in it, rather than late comers who dislike it. There is a strange similarity between the middle-of-the-roaders who disliked fundamentalism in the past and those who dislike fundamentalism in our day.[1]

Today's Questions

Some Fundamentalists are asking these and more basic questions today. A recent meeting of some Fundamentalist pastors featured a lengthy discussion concerning the nature of Fundamentalism. The men concluded that the essential, distinguishing feature of Fundamentalism is separation. Others are asking the same kinds of questions. Charles Wood recounts,

> A correspondent recently indicated that he had been trained in an Independent Baptist Fundamentalist school and had served Independent Baptist Fundamentalist churches for a significant period of time but that he was not aware of having heard a cogent, simple definition of independent Baptist Fundamentalism. He asked if I might be able to provide that definition.[2]

James Singleton, speaking for his generation of leaders, says,

> I have concerns with my generation when we fail to define the core of what constitutes Biblical Fundamentalism, and include as essential in the movement our personal convictions that were never a part of Biblical and

[1]Chester E. Tulga, "The Fundamentalism of Yesterday, the Evangelicalism of Today, and the Fundamentalism of Tomorrow," *Testimonies*, May 1998, p. 7.
[2]Charles Wood, *Pastoral Epistle* (South Bend, IN: personal publication), June 1998, p. 5.

historic Fundamentalism. The result is unnecessary divisions.[3]

Another generation of Fundamentalists is genuinely seeking to understand exactly what the movement is. Singleton seems to indicate that the older generation may not always have been clear in defining itself. These kinds of questions occupy the "front burner" today and deserve answers.

Although Fundamentalism as a movement is a late nineteenth- and twentieth-century phenomenon, its roots run much deeper than that. If we wish to truly understand Fundamentalism, we must go to the Scriptures. This book will assume the burden of proving that Jude's description of New Testament Christianity bears an amazing resemblance to modern-day Fundamentalism as men commonly understand, analyze, and define it.

The Impetus for This Book

In December of 1997, Dr. Frank Bumpus called me and asked me to speak at the 1998 Fundamental Baptist Fellowship national meeting. He assigned me the topic "Stand for Fundamentalism . . . and Against Attempts to Change It." Immediately I began to ask myself the same questions we have noted that others are asking. What really is Fundamentalism? If we do not want to change Fundamental-ism, what is it that we do not want to change?

These questions led to some preliminary investigation of what scholars have written about us. I found, and we will shortly see, a variety of analyses of Fundamentalism. These analyses come from observers who span the theological spectrum from liberal to Fundamentalist. Though each analysis has its own distinctive, a thread of common elements runs

[3]James E. Singleton, "Tensions Between Older and Younger Fundamentalists!" *Whetstone*, May 1998, p. 4.

through the various "takes" on Fundamentalism. I also began to look at the Epistle of Jude, for it calls us to "earnestly contend for the faith which was once delivered unto the saints" (Jude 3). Just as Fundamentalists did battle with unbelievers who infiltrated their denominations, Jude opposed and exposed first-century apostates who infiltrated local churches.

Two sources gave shape to this study. The first was a statement about Fundamentalism from Dr. William Ward Ayer, an earlier Fundamentalist. We will see that statement in a few pages. The other forming source was a commentary on Jude. D. Edmond Hiebert emphasizes that Jude has both a negative and a positive purpose for his book. The negative purpose is to expose false teachers and warn readers about them. Jude's positive purpose is to encourage his readers to "earnestly contend for the faith."[4] Hiebert's point is that Jude not only exposes the nature of error but also teaches the essence of the biblical Christianity that opposes error. As I discovered Jude's positive description of New Testament Christianity, I was amazed and thrilled to see how much it parallels the various analyses of Fundamentalism. We will follow this train of thought.

What Is Liberalism?

We have already referred to the unbelievers who infiltrated the major denominations late in the nineteenth century. These attacks of liberalism roused Bible believers to oppose their teaching. Those Bible believers who stood against the invading liberalism eventually called themselves Fundamentalists. Since we will refer repeatedly to this conflict, we need a concise understanding of what liberalism was and is.

---

[4]D. Edmond Hiebert, *Second Peter and Jude: An Expositional Commentary* (Greenville, SC: Unusual Publications, 1989), p. 203.

Liberalism, or modernism as it was preached in local churches, emphasized five major points:

1. God's character is one of pure benevolence—benevolence, that is, without standards. All men are His children, and sin separates no one from His love. The Fatherhood of God and the brotherhood of man are alike universal.
2. There is a divine spark in every man. All men, therefore, are good at heart and need nothing more than encouragement to allow their natural goodness to express itself.
3. Jesus Christ is man's Savior only in the sense that He is man's perfect teacher and example. We should regard Him simply as the first Christian, our elder brother in the worldwide family of God. He was not divine in any unique sense.
4. Just as Christ differs from other men only comparatively, not absolutely, so Christianity differs from other religions not generically, but as the best and highest type of religion that has yet appeared.
5. The Bible is not a divine record of revelation, but a human testament of religion; and Christian doctrine is not the God-given Word that must create and control Christian experience.[5]

The Purpose of This Study

Our purpose is to discover some objective characteristics of Fundamentalism that take root, not in a movement and its historical evolution, but in the Word of God. We intend to show that Jude's description of New Testament Christianity bears an uncanny resemblance to modern-day Fundamental-

---

[5]J. I. Packer, *"Fundamentalism" and the Word of God* (Grand Rapids: Wm. B. Eerdmans Publishing Company, 1962), pp. 25-26.

ism. The revealed characteristics of first-century Christianity should lay the groundwork for our ministries at the dawning of the twenty-first century.

Not a History
This book will not be a history of Fundamentalism. Friends and foes of Fundamentalism have studied and written its history. We will, necessarily, look at some facts of history. We will look at how the historians have analyzed Fundamentalism. But our primary purpose is to see the biblical basis for Fundamentalism.

Not an Analysis
This study will not attempt to analyze current leaders or the state of the movement. If we can identify the biblical basis for Fundamentalism, then the logical issue will not be what we currently *are* but what we *should be* under the authority of Scripture. We may need to change to get back into conformity with an objective, biblical standard.

The Method of This Study
We will begin by looking together at some representative analyses of Fundamentalism. Liberals, New Evangelicals, and Fundamentalists alike have studied our movement. Some of their work is objective, some is friendly to Fundamentalism, and some is clearly antagonistic. We will identify the common elements these analyses find in Fundamentalism. We will then look at Jude's positive description of New Testament Christianity. The close parallel between Jude's five main characteristics of first-century Christianity and the movement we call Fundamentalism will be obvious.

The Challenge Before Us

This is primarily a self-study. We who gladly claim the title (or epithet as some would have it) of Fundamentalism need to examine our own ministries. Scripture taught, rebuked, corrected, and challenged me as I studied this subject. Some will find weakness in their ministry and life that Scripture does not justify. Some will find spiritual coldness and deadness that the Bible rebukes. Let us submit to Scripture's authority and shape our life by that authority to the glory of our God.

Some will read this work who have little tolerance for Fundamentalism as a movement. Our challenge to you is simple: Let the Word of God speak in all its authority. The Bible sets the parameters for ministry and life. We see a renewed emphasis today on expository preaching. That emphasis prevails in both Fundamentalist and Evangelical circles. Since God's Word is an inspired, authoritative message, we must preach it with clarity and certainty. Since the Word of God is authoritative, we must also obey it in our lives and in our ministries. Submission to the authority of Scripture will produce the same opposition to false teachers it produced in Jude. It will bring biblical condemnation of false teachers rather than the cooperation with them that has so weakened evangelical Christianity in the last half of the twentieth century. Let God's Word govern your life and your ministry.

WHAT IS FUNDAMENTALISM?

> O wad some power the giftie gie us
> To see oursel's as ithers see us!
> It wad frae monie a blunder free us,
> And foolish notion:
> What airs in dress an' gait wad lea'e us
> And ev'n devotion!
>
> –Robert Burns, "To a Louse"

Robert Burns's words whimsically remind us that we need to evaluate ourselves periodically. The poem, "To a Louse," bears a subtitle that reads "On Seeing One on a Lady's Bonnet at Church"! Apparently, several characters in this incident needed to see themselves as others saw them. Burns shows us that Jenny had no idea how silly she looked with the louse parading across her finery. It seems the preacher could have used a good dose of objective evaluation as well. Perhaps the worship was dull and the preaching quite boring that Lord's Day if a louse could so capture the poet's attention! We *really do* need to see ourselves as others see us.

This chapter is going to examine several evaluations of Fundamentalism from history. As we see scholarly evaluations of how this movement began and what distinguished it from the beginning, we can learn much. Dominant traits appear that become the "irreducible minimum" in describing Fundamentalism.

Scripture declares that David "served his own generation by the will of God" (Acts 13:36). Under-standing the classic distinctives of Fundamentalism from generations past will enable us to maintain a balance and sense of direction as we seek to serve the Lord in our own generation. Perhaps we can also avoid some of the "blunders and foolish notions" of which Burns wrote.

A Brief Overview

Larry Pettegrew has succinctly described the historic use of the term "Fundamentalist":

> Actually, the term, "fundamentalist," was first used of a movement in the July 1, 1920, issue of *The Watchman Examiner*. The editor, Curtis Lee Laws, was suggesting possible terms to describe a group of Bible-believing Baptists in the Northern Baptist Convention which was opposing a growing apostasy in the Convention. He concluded his search for a good name by saying: "We suggest that those who still cling to the great fundamentals and who mean to do battle royal for the fundamentals shall be called 'Fundamentalists.' "[1]

Pettegrew, and Curtis Lee Laws before him, saw two elements in nascent Fundamentalism. The movement contains at least a doctrinal element ("the fundamentals") and a militant element ("do battle royal"). Rolland D. McCune sees three major elements in Fundamentalism today, which he names "crucial doctrine," "the distinctive of militancy," and "the distinctive of ecclesiastical separation."[2]

Fundamentalism's Doctrinal Development

The "fundamentals" were variously defined as the Fundamentalist movement developed. One of the first doctrinal formulations of what believers deemed fundamental to the faith

[1]Larry D. Pettegrew, "Will the Real Fundamentalist Please Stand Up?" *Central Testimony*, fall 1982, pp. 1-2.

[2]Rolland D. McCune, "The Self-Identity of Fundamentalism," *Detroit Baptist Seminary Journal*, spring 1996, pp. 9-34.

came from the Niagara Bible Conference in 1878. The Confession of Faith listed fourteen articles:

1. The verbal, plenary inspiration of the Scriptures in the original manuscripts.
2. The Trinity.
3. The Creation of man, the Fall into sin, and total depravity.
4. The universal transmission of spiritual death from Adam.
5. The necessity of the new birth.
6. Redemption by the blood of Christ.
7. Salvation by faith alone in Christ.
8. The assurance of salvation.
9. The centrality of Jesus Christ in the Scriptures.
10. The constitution of the true church by genuine believers.
11. The personality of the Holy Spirit.
12. The believer's call to a holy life.
13. The immediate passing of the souls of believers to be with Christ at death.
14. The premillennial Second Coming of Christ.[3]

From this beginning, further revisions emerged. The most well-known listing is the famous "five fundamentals," which are commonly cited today. Pettegrew describes their origin and content:

> The 1910 General Assembly of the Northern Presbyterian Church listed the following five: (1) Inerrancy, (2) Virgin Birth, (3) Substitutional Atonement, (4) Bodily Resurrection, and (5) Authenticity of Miracles. Later fundamentalists usually combined number five with one of the first

---

[3]Ibid., p. 21, cited from David O. Beale, *In Pursuit of Purity: American Fundamentalism Since 1850* (Greenville, SC: Unusual Publications, 1986), pp. 375-79.

four and included some statement on the second coming of Christ.[4]

These doctrinal "fundamentals" will be referred to regularly in this book.

Non-Fundamentalist Descriptions of Fundamentalism

Many scholars who disavow Fundamentalism have objectively analyzed the movement. Their work deserves attention as we consider how unbelievers understand Fundamentalists and how brethren who do not share Fundamentalist convictions see us.

James Barr

James Barr distances himself from the movement and clearly states that he does not believe in the inerrancy of the Scriptures.[5] He recognizes three major characteristics of Fundamentalism:

(a) "A very strong emphasis on the inerrancy of the Bible, the absence from it of any sort of error";

(b) "A strong hostility to modern theology and to the methods, results, and implications of modern critical study of the Bible"; and

(c) "An assurance that those who do not share their religious viewpoint are not really 'true Christians' at all."[6]

Carl F. H. Henry

Carl F. H. Henry was an early leader in New Evangelicalism. His 1947 book, *The Uneasy Conscience of Modern Fundamentalism*, revealed dissatisfaction with Fundamentalism that

---

[4]Pettegrew, p. 5.
[5]James Barr, *Fundamentalism* (Philadelphia: The Westminster Press, 1977), p. 8.
[6]Ibid., p. 1.

later produced New Evangelicalism. He served on the first faculty at Fuller Theological Seminary and as the first editor of *Christianity Today*. Henry also analyzed Fundamentalism. Henry sees the movement in terms of its separatism:

> Modern prejudice, justly or unjustly, had come to identify Fundamentalism largely in terms of an anti-ecumenical spirit of independent isolationism, an uncritically held set of theological formulas, an overly emotional type of revivalism.[7]

Henry also sees supernaturalism in the movement:

> Fundamentalism was a Bible-believing Christianity which regarded the supernatural as a part of the essence of the Biblical view: the miraculous was not to be viewed, as in liberalism, as an incidental and superfluous accretion.[8]

Henry further identifies militancy as an ingredient of Fundamentalism:

> This is not to suggest that Fundamentalism had no militant opposition to sin. Of all modern viewpoints, when measured against the black background of human nature disclosed by the generation of two world wars, Fundamentalism provided the most realistic appraisal of the condition of man.[9]

George Marsden

George Marsden has taught at Calvin College, the University of California at Berkeley, and Duke University.[10]

---

[7]Carl F. H. Henry, *The Uneasy Conscience of Modern Fundamentalism* (Grand Rapids: Wm. B. Eerdmans Publishing Company, 1947), p. 19.

[8]Ibid.

[9]Ibid., p. 20.

[10]George Marsden, *Reforming Fundamentalism: Fuller Seminary and the New Evangelicalism* (Grand Rapids: William B. Eerdmans Publishing Company, 1987), pp. xi, xii.

Presently he teaches at Notre Dame. He describes Fundamentalism as militantly anti-modernist:

> Briefly, it was militantly anti-modernist Protestant evangelicalism. Fundamentalists were evangelical Christians, . . . who in the twentieth century militantly opposed both modernism in theology and the cultural changes that modernism endorsed. Militant opposition to modernism was what most clearly set off fundamentalism from a number of closely related traditions.[11]

In another work Marsden reaffirms this definition of early Fundamentalism, adding that it exhibited tendencies toward several elements, including separatism and dispensationalism. He points out that detractors would accuse a Fundamentalist of being "obscurantist, anti-intellectual, or a political extremist. So when I speak of fundamentalism here, I do not use the word in such pejorative senses."[12]

Ernest Sandeen

Ernest Sandeen is less complete in his definition, but he also begins,

> A firm trust and belief in every word of the Bible in an age when skepticism was the rule and not the exception—this has been both the pride and the scandal of Fundamentalism. Faith in an inerrant Bible as much as an expectation of the second advent of Christ has been the hallmark of the Fundamentalist.[13]

Sandeen, himself a liberal, understands the importance of an inerrant Bible to Fundamentalism. As he describes the advances of the higher criticism and modernism, he puts the issue in clear focus:

---

[11]George Marsden, *Fundamentalism and American Culture* (Oxford: Oxford University Press, 1980), p. 4.

[12]Marsden, *Reforming Fundamentalism*, p. 10.

[13]Ernest R. Sandeen, *The Roots of Fundamentalism* (Grand Rapids: Baker Book House, 1970), p. 103.

When many others carried on, supported by their personal experience or faith in the church, why did some Christians demand an inerrant Bible? *This is the central question of Fundamentalist historiography* [emphasis mine].[14]

Sandeen also understands the importance of premillennialism to the Fundamentalist movement. He continues:

The understanding of millenarian hermeneutics—the manner in which the millenarians interpreted the Bible— and the theology of biblical authority developed at Princeton Seminary in the nineteenth century can help to answer this question.[15]

Grant Wacker

Grant Wacker, writing about Augustus Hopkins Strong and his attempt to balance biblical orthodoxy with invading modernism, understands the issues in a similar way:

Fundamentalism is used in a still more restricted fashion to designate the militant emphasis on the inerrancy of the Bible and the deity and miracles of Jesus Christ that emerged in the early twentieth century in opposition to theological modernism.[16]

A Summary

Non-Fundamentalists commonly identify several traits of Fundamentalism. They see the following:

1. An emphasis on the inspiration, infallibility, inerrancy, and authority of the Bible.
2. An opposition to modernism.
3. An emphasis on separatism.
4. A belief in the premillennial return of Christ.

---

[14]Ibid., p. 107.

[15]Ibid.

[16]Grant Wacker, *Augustus H. Strong and the Dilemma of Historical Consciousness* (Macon, GA: Mercer University Press, 1985), p. 18.

5. An opposition to sin and the cultural decay produced by modernism.

6. A militant spirit.

Fundamentalist Descriptions of Fundamentalism

Fundamentalists have also spent extensive time analyzing their own movement. Their descriptions of Fundamentalism are strikingly similar to the Liberal and New Evangelical descriptions.

William Ward Ayer

Speaking to the National Association of Evangelicals in 1956, William Ward Ayer put the term into historical perspective:

> Fundamentalism represents a resurgence of ancient practices, which began not with Martin Luther but at Pentecost. Fundamentalism is apostolic, and the doctrine of justification goes back to Paul. That branch from which the fundamentalist movement sprang lived obscurely through the ages and had never been completely silenced even in the Dark Ages. . . . What fundamentalism did was to awaken the slumbering apostolicism from lethargy. The theme of the Reformation, like the cry of the fundamentalists today, was "back to the Bible and the Apostles," with no mediator between men and God except Christ. Fundamentalists are in the direct line of succession to those preaching this same message.[17]

This statement deserves serious consideration and will be the point of departure for this book. Ayer is right! Certain distinctives have marked Fundamentalists because those distinctives come from the Word of God.

---

[17]William Ward Ayer, speech to the National Association of Evangelicals, April 1956, quoted in Louis Gasper, *The Fundamentalist Movement, 1930-1956* (1963; reprint, Grand Rapids: Baker Book House, 1981), pp. 2-3.

David Beale

In his definitive history of Fundamentalism, David Beale states,

> Ideally, a Christian Fundamentalist is one who desires to reach out in love and compassion to people, believes and defends the whole Bible as the absolute, inerrant, and authoritative Word of God, and stands committed to the doctrine and practice of holiness. . . . Fundamentalism is not a philosophy of Christianity, nor is it essentially an interpretation of the Scriptures. It is not even a mere literal exposition of the Bible. The essence of Fundamentalism goes much deeper than that—it is the *unqualified acceptance of and obedience to the Scriptures* [emphasis Beale's].[18]

David Cummins

David Cummins, Baptist pastor, author, and now deputation director for Baptist World Mission, defines Fundamentalism in similar fashion:

> A fundamentalist is one who believes in the literal interpretation of the Scriptures leading to a pre-millennial eschatology. This distinctive causes him, like Jude, to earnestly contend for the faith, to preach and teach with certitude the full counsel of the Word of God, to promote evangelism and practice worldwide missions. Simultaneously, such a one is impelled like Paul to ecclesiastical separatism and a militancy in opposing false teaching, evangelistic compromise, and the apostasy. In like manner, a fundamentalist practices personal separation from worldliness in all of its various expressions and a personal commitment to a life of holiness.[19]

---

[18]David O. Beale, *In Pursuit of Purity: American Fundamentalism Since 1850* (Greenville, SC: Unusual Publications, 1986), p. 3.

[19]David L. Cummins, in personal correspondence, April 13, 1998.

Robert Delnay

Robert Delnay is a Baptist church historian. He has served as a professor in several institutions, most recently at Clearwater Christian College. His research on the Baptist Bible Union yielded an extensive analysis of the Fundamentalist movement. Delnay identifies the following distinctives of the movement:

1. Biblicism—inerrancy and biblical authority
2. Separatism
3. Premillennialism
4. Conviction, militancy
5. Spirituality—"Biblical, spiritual contact with the unseen God"
6. Evangelism
7. Confidence in the power of preaching
8. Distrust of secular education
9. Interdenominationalism[20]

Bob Jones Jr.

"Dr. Bob," as he was affectionately known, was probably Fundamentalism's leading spokesman in recent years. He captured the essence of the movement's commitment to Scripture and its militancy with these words:

> A Fundamentalist is a person who is soundly converted and born again through faith in the blood of Christ, who believes the Bible is God's Word, who is willing to defend the Scripture with his life's blood, who preaches and proclaims the Word, and who seeks to obey it.[21]

---

[20]Robert Delnay, "Distinctive Marks of Fundamentalism" (Clearwater Christian College, lecture notes), 2 pages.

[21]Bob Jones Jr., "As I See It," *Preach the Word*, January-March 1998, p. 12.

Larry Pettegrew

Pettegrew, then acting dean of Central Seminary, commented on Fundamentalism's beginnings, as we have noted. He went on to list several of its distinguishing marks. First, he identified it as a movement with "a distinct name, a distinct theology, distinct churches, distinct leaders, distinct literature, and distinct educational institutions."[22] He also identified Fundamentalism's affirmation of the previously noted five fundamentals of the faith. He then identified Fundamentalism's militancy, and finally, he described the movement's emphasis on separatism, saying,

> What does all this tell us about the modern fundamentalist movement? Without question, ecclesiastical separation has *rightly* become a more important aspect of the fundamentalist movement in recent years. Some would even say that it has become *the* distinctive [emphasis Pettegrew's].[23]

Major Distinctives of Fundamentalism

We easily observe widespread agreement about the essential nature of Fundamentalism. Those who have written from a Fundamentalist perspective arrive at several common conclusions about the movement. They identify the following major distinctives:

1. Fundamentalists stand for the Bible as the supernaturally revealed, inspired Word of God.
2. Fundamentalists embrace a doctrinal frame of reference, most commonly identified by "five fundamentals."

---

[22]Pettegrew, p. 2.
[23]Ibid. We note that Pettegrew now teaches at The Master's Seminary, where ecclesiastical separation is not emphasized as Pettegrew emphasized it in this article.

The 1910 General Assembly of the Northern Presbyterian Church first articulated this formulation.

3. Fundamentalists show a militant opposition to apostasy, otherwise known as modernism or liberalism.

4. Separatism is a major distinctive of Fundamentalism.

5. Fundamentalism has been, from the beginning, an interdenominational movement.

6. A premillennial viewpoint is prominent in Fundamentalism, though this is not a test of fellowship.

Fundamentalism and Premillennialism

The issue of the premillennial rapture deserves comment. We list premillennialism as a distinctive of the movement because from the 1878 Niagara Confession of Faith forward, many held this view of the Lord's return. Liberals such as Sandeen, as well as several Fundamentalists, list it as distinctive of the movement. It is important to understand that not all Fundamentalists are premillennial, nor is it necessary to hold the premillennial view of Christ's return to be considered a Fundamentalist. Nevertheless, premillennialism is prominent in the movement. Beale says, "Most Fundamentalists agreed on a general premillennial scheme of eschatology but agreed to disagree—at least for a time—on minute details."[24]

Fundamentalism and Interdenominationalism

We have already seen that Fundamentalism places primary emphasis on the supernatural character of the Bible as God's revelation to the human race. We will develop that Fundamentalist belief in the next chapter. It is safe to say that Fundamentalists are what they are because they believe Scripture to be a revelation from God, written by inspiration of the

---

[24]Beale, p. 27.

Holy Spirit. That conviction is the Fundamentalists' foundation—it is our very reason for being.

We who are Baptists are quick to assert that the very same tenet, the authority of Scripture, is also the reason we are Baptists. The same Word that teaches us our doctrine also mandates our practice. Chester E. Tulga stated, "The basic tenet of the historic Baptist faith is that the Bible is the Word of God and the sole authority of faith and practice."[25] British pastor and historian Jack Hoad states, "It is the Biblical doctrine of the church, with an unqualified submission to Scripture as the Word of God, which becomes the test of what is a Baptist church."[26] "The Baptist is a Scripture-ruled believer."[27] In the New Testament, we find that local churches were independent of any outside controlling authority. They enjoyed a voluntary, fraternal relationship with one another (Acts 15:1-35). We find that only saved people became members of New Testament churches (Acts 2:47). The New Testament teaches only two officers in the local church—pastors and deacons (I Tim. 3:1-13)—and only two symbolic ordinances—baptism and the Lord's Supper (Rom. 6:3-5; I Cor. 11:23-34). Scripture declares that each believer is a priest before God and has direct access into the presence of God through the blood of Christ (I Pet. 2:9; Heb. 10:19-22). Jesus taught that the Christian lives in two frames of reference—"Caesar's" and "God's" (Matt. 22:20-21). Therefore, we believe the church and the state should be separate. We hold that these issues of church practice (commonly called the Baptist distinctives when combined) come from and are mandated by Scripture.

---

[25]Chester E. Tulga, "What Baptists Believe About Soul Liberty," *The Baptist Challenge*, October 1997, p. 21.

[26]Jack Hoad, *The Baptist* (London: Grace Publications Trust, 1986), p. 7.

[27]Ibid., p. 225.

Having said that, we must understand that Fundamentalism began as an interdenominational movement. Christians who believed the Bible and opposed modernism set aside their denominational distinctives to come together and lift a united voice for those truths that made up the "irreducible minimum" of Christianity. They fought against liberalism in their own denominations and also united outside denominational frameworks to fight against it. Richard Harris, himself a Baptist, explains the thinking of most Fundamentalists on this issue:

> There have always been honest differences of interpretation on church organization, as well as on other issues, among good men who love Christ. There was a time when men could amicably differ on issues which did not affect fundamental Christian doctrine and still respect and firmly defend one another. Great Christian leaders of the past were able to respect those differences and yet recognize that the men with whom they differed were still Fundamentalists and brothers in Christ. They were Christian statesmen.[28]

Speaking of the formation of the American Council of Christian Churches in 1941, Harris goes on:

> It made no difference that some of them were Baptist, some were Evangelical Methodists, some were Bible Presbyterians, and some of other persuasions. Their fellowship was characterized by their common belief that the Bible is the authoritative, inerrant Word of God. All of them believed in the Virgin Birth, the Deity of Christ, His substitutionary atonement for sin, His bodily resurrection and ascension into Heaven and His coming again in power and glory. Each believed the Bible taught that the Church should be separate from apostasy and Christians should be obedient to Christ.[29]

---

[28]Richard A. Harris, "A Plea for Christian Statesmanship," *The Challenge*, December 1997, p. 1.

[29]Ibid., p. 2.

The early Fundamentalists represented many denominational traditions, and Fundamentalism was an interdenominational movement. There should still be a place for Fundamentalists of various persuasions to come together and stand together for "the faith once delivered to the saints" (Jude 3) and against "certain men crept in unawares" (Jude 4). The American Council of Christian Churches still performs a legitimate service. It is still proper for the International Testimony to an Infallible Bible to call Fundamentalists from around the world to stand united in a World Congress of Fundamentalists. We need to help and encourage each other.

Moderating Voices

Jerry Falwell

The last twenty years have produced various attempts to change the face of historic Fundamentalism. Jerry Falwell was one of the first who attempted to change the perception of Fundamentalism. His publication at that time, the *Fundamentalist Journal*, defined the movement solely in terms of the classic "five fundamentals."[30] In another place, Edward Dobson and Ed Hindson stated, "Doctrinally, Fundamentalism is really traditional and conservative Christian orthodoxy."[31] Later, Falwell did speak of ecclesiastical separation, but only about being "free from hierarchical structures that would tie us down to denominational mediocrity."[32] The militant element seems to be missing from Falwell's description of Fundamentalism. In more recent years, Falwell appears to have forsaken the term and the movement.

[30]Edward Dobson, "I Am Proud to Be a Fundamentalist," *Fundamentalist Journal*, June 1985, p. 12.

[31]Jerry Falwell, ed., *The Fundamentalist Phenomenon* (Garden City, NY: Doubleday & Company, Inc., 1981), p. 11.

[32]Ibid., p. 220.

23

Charles Colson

Charles Colson defines the term similarly in his book *The Body*. He tells how he was accused in a *New York Times* article of being a Fundamentalist. He then says,

> There's the dreaded word. It conjures up images of uneducated bigots, backward Bible-thumping preachers, and the Ayatollah Ruhollah Khomeni. But it's a bad rap.

> "Fundamentalism" is really akin to Lewis's "mere Christianity" discussed earlier, or the rules of faith in the early church; it means adherence to the fundamental facts—in this case, the fundamental facts of Christianity. It is a term that was once a badge of honor, and we should reclaim it.[33]

Colson goes on to describe the birth of the movement and the struggle with modernism. He describes how Bible-believing Christians identified the "five fundamentals" as "the infallibility of Scripture, the deity of Christ, the Virgin Birth and miracles of Christ, Christ's substitutionary death, and Christ's physical resurrection and eventual return."[34] Setting aside any understanding that Fundamentalism today shows any militance against or separation from apostasy, Colson makes this astounding statement:

> These were then, as they are today, the backbone of orthodox Christianity. If a fundamentalist is a person who affirms these truths, then there are fundamentalists in every denomination—Catholic, Presbyterian, Baptist, Brethren, Methodist, Episcopal. . . . *Everyone who believes in the orthodox truths about Jesus Christ—in short, every Christian—is a fundamentalist.* And we should not shrink from the term nor allow the secular world to distort its meaning [emphasis mine].[35]

---

[33]Charles Colson, *The Body* (Dallas: Word Publishing, 1992), p. 161.
[34]Ibid, p. 162.
[35]Ibid.

Colson has correctly identified the fundamental doctrines around which early Fundamentalists rallied. Certainly every born-again Christian believes these truths about Christ. He is probably correct that there are believers in many denominational bodies who believe those doctrines. However, Colson either ignores or is unaware of the history of the movement that calls itself "Fundamentalism." He completely ignores the militant aspect in Fundamentalism. He is widely divergent from Curtis Lee Laws's first definition of the term. Harold John Ockenga, Carl F. H. Henry, Kenneth Kantzer, and others who split the New Evangelicalism out of the Fundamentalist movement of the 1940s would vigorously disagree with Colson on this point.[36] They were frustrated with Fundamentalism because they disliked its separation.

We have looked at serious and thoughtful descriptions of Fundamentalism. The fact emerges that no serious student of the movement, regardless of his theological orientation, will agree with either Falwell or Colson. Those who have studied Fundamentalism universally describe a militant opposition in the movement to false doctrine and to apostate denial of the fundamentals of the faith. Fundamentalism is a doctrinal movement, but it is far more than that. These attempts to redefine or "dumb down" Fundamentalism fly in the face of

---

[36]Note, for instance, that Harold John Ockenga, in his press release December 8, 1957 (Boston: The Park Street Church), stated, "The strategy of the New Evangelicalism has changed from one of separation to infiltration." Two paragraphs later he said, "The New Evangelicalism is willing to face the intellectual problems and meet them in the framework of modern learning. It stands doctrinally upon the creeds and confessions of the Church and grants liberty in minor areas when discussion is promoted on the basis of exegesis of Scripture." Ockenga insisted that the New Evangelicalism would retain orthodox doctrine but renounce Fundamentalism's militancy and separatism. The first generation New Evangelicalism divided from Fundamentalism over separation. Believers who remain in apostate churches and denominations reflect the New Evangelical, *not* the Fundamentalist, philosophy. History demonstrates that Colson's description is clearly *not* an accurate understanding of Fundamentalism.

history and the thoughtful analysis of many students, whether friend or foe of the movement.

Conclusion

Our conclusion in this chapter is quite simple. Liberals, New Evangelicals, and Fundamentalists alike find many common marks in the movement we call Fundamentalism. They almost universally identify Fundamentalism's beginning point as faith in the Bible as God's revealed Word. Militance in opposing religious liberalism (that movement that denies the divine inspiration, authority, and doctrines of the Bible) is a second distinguishing mark. Many writers see a resulting separation from unbelief as a trait that developed within Fundamentalism. Premillennialism and interdenominationalism were other features of this movement.

Ayer seems to have put the issue in perspective. He identifies Fundamentalism as an expression of apostolic Christianity. The rest of this book will turn to the Epistle of Jude. As we see Jude's description of Apostolic and New Testament-era Christianity, the parallels between first-century Christianity and twentieth-century Fundamentalism will amaze us.

THE FUNDAMENTALISTS' FOUNDATION

Part I

How firm a foundation, ye saints of the Lord,
Is laid for your faith in His excellent Word!
What more can He say than to you He hath said,
To you who for refuge to Jesus have fled?[1]

Beloved, when I gave all diligence to write unto you of
the common salvation, it was needful for me to write unto
you, and exhort you that ye should earnestly contend for
the faith which was once delivered unto the saints
(Jude 3).

Jude's original intent was to write an epistle concerning
"the common salvation." "But he found it necessary to warn
his readers concerning innovators who were smuggling false
teaching into the churches."[2] In warning first-century believers against these false teachers, Jude also positively describes
the nature of genuine New Testament Christianity. His first
statement explaining true Christianity tells us of "the faith
which was once delivered unto the saints" (v. 3). Jude's definition of New Testament Christianity begins with an affirmation that God has revealed His Word to men. We have
looked at many analyses of Fundamentalism. Those studies
universally begin by acknowledging that Fundamentalism
rests on a belief that the Bible is the inspired, inerrant Word
of God. Fundamentalism's foundation is not an accident. Fundamentalists begin to articulate their faith precisely where

---

[1]Rippon's Selection, 1787, "How Firm a Foundation."
[2]Edwin A. Blum, "Jude" in Frank E. Gaebelein, ed., *The Expositor's Bible Commentary* (Grand Rapids: Zondervan Publishing House, 1981), 12:384.

Scripture begins. In this chapter we will examine Jude's statement concerning the Bible.

Satan's Ploy

As we begin looking at Jude's discussion of Scripture, we should realize that Jude is fighting a battle in an ages-old war. Satan's tactics have not changed since the Garden of Eden. When God created Adam and Eve, He did not leave them to discover their own way on the earth. He gave them a mandate to reproduce and to have dominion over the physical creation (Gen. 1:28). He also instructed them concerning their food (Gen. 1:29). Beyond that, God forbade them to eat of the tree of the knowledge of good and evil (Gen. 2:16-18). Scripture tells us how Adam and Eve learned how to live. They did not discover truth by their powers of observation. They did not arrive at certain conclusions by reason. Scripture tells us that *"God said"* (Gen. 1:28, 29) and that *"the Lord God commanded the man"* (Gen. 2:16). God clearly revealed His will for the human race to Adam. To say it another way, *Adam learned truth by revelation from God!*

When Satan came to tempt Eve, he approached her with the question "Yea, hath God said?" (Gen. 3:1). His first attack against God and His creation on earth was aimed at raising doubts about God's revelation to men. Satan has never changed his tactics. He has continually attacked the veracity and reliability of God's Word. Thus the Holy Spirit leads Jude to begin his description of biblical Christianity with an affirmation that "the faith" is a revelation from God.

The Faith

New Testament authors, writing by inspiration of the Holy Spirit, repeatedly use the term "the faith" in their writings. "Faith" describes the sinner's trust in Christ alone for salvation and the believer's resultant trust in God and His Word. A believer's faith produces obedience to God (e.g., Heb. 11:4, 7, 8). "The faith" is a term frequently used by the Holy Spirit to identify the substance of Christianity. Lovik describes the term as "the whole body of truth given to them by the apostles."[3] Vine calls it "what is believed, the contents of belief, the faith."[4] Alford calls it "the sum of that which Christians believe."[5] Lenski elaborates: "*pistis* is often undoubtedly the faith *which* one believes, the doctrine, teaching, creed, gospel, divine truth (objective). It is so here in Jude, also in Phil. 1:27" [emphasis Lenski's].[6] Morris states, " 'The faith' is not in reference to the simple trust we place in Christ in salvation, but to the entire body of Christian truth as revealed in the Holy Scriptures."[7]

In several passages Scripture uses this term, "the faith," of the body of truth accepted by Christians. Paul urges the Philippian believers to be "striving together for *the faith* of the gospel" (Phil. 1:27). He equates the gospel and *"the faith."* He teaches Timothy that deacons must hold "the mystery of *the faith* in a pure conscience" (I Tim. 3:9). He warns him that "some shall depart from *the faith*, giving heed to seducing

---

[3]Gordon Lovik, "These Men in Your Church, An Exegesis of the Book of Jude" (Minneapolis: Central C. B. Seminary, n.d.), p. 29.

[4]W. E. Vine, *An Expository Dictionary of New Testament Words* (Westwood, NJ: Fleming H. Revell Company, 1966 edition), II:71.

[5]Henry Alford, *The Greek New Testament* (Cambridge: Deighton, Bell and Company, 1862), IV:530.

[6]R.C.H. Lenski, *I and II Epistles of Peter, the Three Epistles of John, and the Epistle of Jude* (Minneapolis: Augsburg Publishing House, 1966), p. 610.

[7]Henry M. Morris, *The Defender's Study Bible* (Grand Rapids: World Publications, Inc., 1995), p. 1423.

spirits, and doctrines of devils" (I Tim. 4:1). False doctrine stands in antithesis to "the faith." When he closes his first epistle to Timothy, he commands him to "fight the good fight of *the faith*" (I Tim. 6:12) and sadly reports that some "have erred concerning *the faith*" (1 Tim. 6:21). In his farewell, after urging Timothy to "preach the word" (II Tim. 4:2), he can say, "I have fought a good fight, I have finished my course, I have kept *the faith*" (II Tim. 4:7). We can safely say that "the faith" speaks of that body of truth God has revealed to men in His Word.

A Revealed Word

Jude not only describes that for which we are to contend as "the faith," but he also teaches us the source of that faith. It was "once delivered unto the saints" (Jude 3). Christians around the world have trusted Christ because they heard the message of "the faith of the gospel" (Phil. 1:27). They believe "the faith" and obey it because of the unique way in which they received it. "The faith" has been "delivered" to them. This word "delivered" goes to the heart of what the Bible claims to be—specifically, a revelation from God Himself. Unger states, "Revelation is the divine act of communicating to man truth which otherwise man could not know."[8]

A Word of Revelation

The Holy Spirit uses the Greek word *paradidomi*, which has as its primary meaning to "hand over, give (over), deliver, entrust."[9] The noun form of the word, *paradosis*, means "handing down or over" and is often translated "tradition" in

---

[8]Merrill F. Unger, *Introductory Guide to the Old Testament* (Grand Rapids: Zondervan Publishing House, 1956), p. 22.

[9]William F. Arndt and F. Wilbur Gingrich, *A Greek-English Lexicon of the New Testament* (Chicago: The University of Chicago Press, 1957), p. 619.

the New Testament. Scripture uses the terms in various ways. One specific way the New Testament uses these words is to identify truth God has revealed to men. At least five times New Testament authors use the words to describe revealed truth.

Revelation to Paul
    Paul uses the word twice to emphasize that the revelation he gave to the Corinthians came from God. He says, "For I have received of the Lord that which also I delivered unto you" (I Cor. 11:23). Paul *delivered* to the Corinthians, by his apostolic authority, a message he received from the Lord. God revealed truth to Paul. He then used the apostle to "deliver" that truth to the Corinthian church and, thus, to succeeding generations of Christians through the New Testament. Paul uses this formula a second time when he describes the gospel, saying, "For I delivered unto you first of all that which I also received" (I Cor. 15:3). Paul was the human instrument by which God communicated His revealed truth to men.

    Paul also used the word to describe his message to the Thessalonians. He commands them to "stand fast, and hold the traditions which ye have been taught, whether by word, or our epistle" (II Thess. 2:15). This "tradition" was not a mere custom among the early churches. The apostle was not speaking about the time of their Lord's Day services nor of when they gathered for fellowship and prayer. He commanded them to obey what they learned from him as an apostle. That truth is important because it is in his epistle. That truth is re-vealed Scripture.

Revelation in Peter's Writings
    Peter uses the word in the same way. Peter warns us about false teachers who "bring in damnable heresies, even denying the Lord that bought them, and bring upon themselves swift destruction" (II Pet. 2:1). In II Peter 2:21 he says, "For it had

been better for them not to have known the way of righteousness, than, after they have known it, to turn from the holy commandment *delivered* unto them" [emphasis mine]. The use of the term "holy commandment" leaves no doubt that Peter is speaking of the Word of God. These apostates turned from the Scriptures. Peter seems to say that their sin is especially deplorable because they turned from that which God "delivered" or revealed to them. Scripture is not of merely human origin. God revealed it to men.

Revelation in Jude

The servant of Christ and half-brother of our Lord now uses this term in his epistle. Enemies of the faith infiltrated local churches as the New Testament era drew to a close. Believers had to contend for the faith. The faith is precious and must be defended because it is "once delivered to the saints" (Jude 3). This truth, believed by Christians and written in the Christian Scriptures, is revealed truth. God is telling us, through Paul, Peter, and Jude, that the Word of God is His revelation to men.

Revelation in Scripture

Thus far we have followed a very narrow focus on the use of Jude's word *paradosis*. This word, as three New Testament books use it, clearly identifies truth that God has made known to men. Other Scripture also tells us that God has revealed Himself to men. This is a large topic, but we will examine a few instances that outline this teaching.

Kinds of Revelation

The Bible teaches us that God reveals Himself to men in two ways. *General revelation* is how God makes Himself known to all men. People see this general revelation from God in nature. Psalm 19:1-6 declares this truth. Verse one states, "The heavens declare the glory of God; and the firmament showeth his handywork." Paul elaborates on the same point in Romans 1:19, 20:

> Because that which may be known of God is manifest in them; for God hath showed it unto them. For the invisible things of him from the creation of the world are clearly seen, being understood by the things that are made, even his eternal power and Godhead; so that they are without excuse.

Nature reveals God's glory. Nature shows man that God is and that He had the mind to devise and the power to create the world. Thus, man faces the reality that he is God's creature and is "without excuse" (Rom. 1:20) and accountable to God.

God has apparently also carried general revelation to man's conscience. Paul tells us, "For when the Gentiles, which have not the law, do by nature the things contained in the law, these, having not the law, are a law unto themselves" (Rom. 2:14). René Pache summarizes this truth:

> In creating man in His image, God endowed him with a moral and a spiritual sense. The great principles of the divine law are imprinted on his heart: appreciation for the excellence of that which is good, and joy in accomplishing it; also knowledge of the evil that is opposed to the divine will, and a feeling of guilt, desire for justification, and responsibility before the Creator.[10]

Having rejected God's revelation, the human race has plunged itself into blindness and depravity (Rom. 1:21-32). Men are under the judgment of God when they reject God's revelation (Rom. 1:32). Men can and do reject God's revelation. They can so sin against their consciences that they become "seared with a hot iron" (I Tim. 4:2). Nevertheless, God

---

[10]René Pache, *The Inspiration and Authority of Scripture* (Chicago: Moody Press, 1969), p. 16.

has revealed Himself to all men in nature and in their conscience.

God has also given men *special revelation*. The Bible declares that God spoke to men "at sundry times and in divers manners" (Heb. 1:1). Pache lists several means by which God revealed Himself to men, including theophanies (God appearing to men), dreams and visions, direct contact with men, miracles and signs, the prophets, and "the revelation of God in Jesus Christ."[11] God's revelation in Christ is the fulfillment of His revelation in the Law (John 1:17). It shows us the glory of God (John 1:18) and provides salvation for sinful men (John 1:29). Through the process of inspiration, God supernaturally communicated His revelation to men in written form, thus giving us His Word. Moses clearly tells us he understands that what he has written in the Pentateuch is revelation from God. In Deuteronomy 29:29 he states, "The secret things belong unto the Lord our God: but those things which are revealed belong unto us and to our children for ever, that we may do all the words of this law."

David speaks eloquently of God's special revelation in His Word. Writing in Psalm 19:7-11, he tells us,

> The law of the Lord is perfect, converting the soul: the testimony of the Lord is sure, making wise the simple. The statutes of the Lord are right, rejoicing the heart: the commandment of the Lord is pure, enlightening the eyes. The fear of the Lord is clean, enduring for ever: the judgments of the Lord are true and righteous altogether. More to be desired are they than gold, yea, than much fine gold: sweeter also than honey and the honeycomb. Moreover by them is thy servant warned: and in keeping of them there is great reward.

---

[11]Ibid., pp. 20-22.

This revelation from God "turns" or converts the soul, imparts wisdom, rejoices the heart, and gives discernment to those who heed it.

An Authoritative Revelation

These brief descriptions of God's revelation to men show us one other critical point—God's revelation to men is authoritative and therefore is to be obeyed. The Deuteronomy passage tells us that God has given His revelation to us "that we may do all the words of this law" (Deut. 29:29). David tells us that "in keeping of them [God's judgments] there is great reward" (Ps. 19:11). A revealed Word is an authoritative Word that man is bound to obey. God ties the authority of His Word to the fact that it is His revelation. Carl F. H. Henry succinctly summarizes the biblical idea of revelation with two statements:

> Revelation is a divinely initiated activity, God's free communication by which he alone turns his personal privacy into a deliberate disclosure of his reality. . . . Divine revelation is given for human benefit, offering us privileged communion with our Creator in the kingdom of God.[12]

A Completed Revelation

Jude adds one more important truth to his statement about "the faith." He tells us it "was *once* delivered to the saints" (Jude 3) [emphasis mine]. That statement tells us that God's revelation is complete and we need expect no more. The word "once" and its place in the verse bear out our contention.

[12]Carl F. H. Henry, *God, Revelation, and Authority* (Waco, TX: Word Publishing, 1976), II:17, 30.

Delivered Once

The little word "once" in verse three is the Greek word *hapax*, which conveys the meaning of "once for all."[13] The Holy Spirit tells us through Jude that God revealed Himself to us in Scripture ("the faith"), and He completed His revelation. Lenski explains,

> "Once delivered" (effective aorist) means "once for all" (the classical meaning) and not merely "on one occasion."... To offer doctrines that are other than this faith is to offer falsehood, poison. To subtract from or add to this faith is to take away what Christ gave, or to supply what he did not give.[14]

By using this forceful word, Jude surely is telling us that no other revelation will be given.

Emphatic

Jude further emphasizes the fact of a completed revelation by the order in which he uses his words in the sentence. In a Greek text this phrase reads "the once-for-all delivered to the saints faith."[15] This places the primary emphasis in the sentence on the word "once" more than "the faith."

Jude is certainly not de-emphasizing "the faith." It is the substance of God's revelation, believed by Christians and recorded in Scripture. Jude's main emphasis is that "the faith" is a "once for all" revelation. God gave it to us over a period of sixteen hundred years through forty human authors. New Testament Christians received the Old Testament as God's revelation. They also recognized the writings of the apostles as Scripture (II Pet. 3:16). When John the Apostle wrote "Amen" (Rev. 22:21), God's revelation was completed. God

---

[13]Arndt and Gingrich, p. 80.

[14]Lenski, p. 611.

[15]New Testament scholars call this the "first attributive position" where the adjective follows the article and precedes the noun. Daniel B. Wallace, *Greek Grammar Beyond the Basics* (Grand Rapids: Zondervan Publishing House, 1996), p. 306.

has given us "all things that pertain unto life and godliness" (II Pet. 1:3) and He has not changed His mind. He curses those who would add to or subtract from His revelation (Rev. 22:18, 19). Many have attempted to deny, modify, or add to God's Word by one means or another. Jude declares that New Testament Christianity rests on the foundation of a completed revelation from God. Biblical Fundamentalism in the present day stands on the same foundation of a complete revelation from God.

Opposition to God's Revelation

Through the centuries, God's Word has endured countless attacks. Satan's temptation of Eve began with the subtle attack on God's revelation. He asked: "Yea, hath God said?" (Gen. 3:1). B. B. Warfield provides a keen analysis of these attacks on God's Word:

> In the whole history of the church there have been but two movements of thought, tending to a lower conception of the inspiration and authority of Scripture, which have attained sufficient proportions to bring them into view in an historical sketch. (1) The first of these may be called the Rationalistic view.[16]

This rationalistic approach to Scripture has caused great theological battles in the last 150 years. Its roots really grew out of Enlightenment thinking, popularized by Friedrich Schleiermacher at the beginning of the nineteenth century. It emerged as a formalized concept in the 1860s with the Graf-Wellhausen theory, which came out of Heidelberg, Germany. As it developed, this "modernism," as it became known, taught that Moses did not really write the Pentateuch. Rather, some later editor, using four separate sources, "cut and

---

[16]B. B. Warfield, *The Inspiration and Authority of the Bible* (Philadelphia: The Presbyterian and Reformed Publishing Company, 1948), p. 112.

pasted" the Pentateuch together as a reflection of human tradition. Likewise, according to the "higher critics," two or pos-
sibly four separate authors wrote the Book of Isaiah rather
than the prophet of whom the Scriptures speak. The Book of
Daniel looks like it was written as prophecy, but, according to
this "higher criticism," it was really written after the fact.
These allegations have been disproved by historical and
archeological evidence. These false premises have been
through many revisions and finally now have been almost
completely abandoned. A modern form of this folly is the so-
called "Jesus Seminar," which has decided that Jesus actually
spoke about twenty percent of what the Gospels attribute to
Him!

This rationalistic system intended to prove that the Bible
is not a supernatural revelation from God, but merely a
human book containing moral and ethical principles. Based
on evolution, it denied the supernatural character of the Bible
and the miraculous claims the Bible makes. This system of
unbelief spread from the European universities to the denominational universities, colleges, and seminaries in the United
States.

Bible believers in Europe and the United States rose up
in opposition to the attacks of modernism. Spurgeon fought
the famous Down-Grade controversy and eventually withdrew
from the Baptist Union in England over it. Frederick Godet,
the famous Swiss exegete, was a thorough-going Bible believer. In Germany, E. W. Hengstenberg withstood the arguments of Schleiermacher.[17] In the United States those who
believed the Bible vigorously fought against the invading
modernism. Early in this century godly men published a series
of writings in defense of the faith called *The Fundamentals*.

---

[17]Stephan Holthaus, *Fundamentalismus in Deutschland, Der Kampf um die Bibel im Protestantismus des 19. und 20. Jahrhunderts* (Bonn: Verlag für Kultur und Wissenschaft, Dr. Thomas Schirrmacher, 1993), pp.156-60.

Pettegrew documented that Curtis Lee Laws adopted the term "Fundamentalist" for those who believe God's Word and intend to defend it.[18] This is a brief summary of the rationalistic attack on the Scriptures in modern times. Fundamentalism as a movement emerged as a defense against the attacks of modernism.[19]

Please note Warfield's previous statement that opposition to Scripture has followed "two movements of thought."[20] While modernism was a rationalistic attack on the Scriptures, the second type of attack on God's Word is really more prominent today. It demands a more detailed examination. Warfield continued his observation:

> (2) The second of the lowered views of inspiration may be called the Mystical view. Its characteristic conception is that the Christian man has something within himself,—call it enlightened reason, spiritual insight, the Christian consciousness, the witness of the Spirit, or call it what you will,—to the test of which every "external revelation" is to be subjected, and according to the decision of which are the contents of the Bible to be valued.[21]

---

[18]Larry D. Pettegrew, "Will The Real Fundamentalist Please Stand Up?" *Central Testimony*, fall 1982, pp. 1-2.

[19]Mark Sidwell, in *The Dividing Line* (Greenville, SC: Bob Jones University Press, 1998), pp. 91-102, has a comprehensive, clear description of liberalism. Sidwell has done an outstanding job of describing liberalism in historically precise, theologically correct, and yet understandable language.

[20]Warfield, p. 112.

[21]Ibid., p. 113. A. T. Pierson, *Seed Thoughts for Public Speakers* (New York: Funk and Wagnalls Co., 1900), p. 178, made a four-way analysis of religion and authority. He said, "There are four types of religious life: 1. The rationalistic, in which all truth and doctrine are submitted to the reason as the supreme arbiter. 2. The ecclesiastic, in which the Church is practically the final authority. 3. The mystic, in which the "inner light" interprets even Christian doctrine. 4. The evangelic, in which the soul bows to the authority of the inspired Word, and makes the reason, the voice of the Church, and the inner instincts and impulses subordinate, as fallible sources of authority, to the one supreme tribunal of Scripture" [emphasis Pierson's].

This "mystical" approach to Scripture opens the door for the error of continuing revelation.

Continuing Revelation—A Crucial Issue

Jude's affirmation that we have a completed revelation from God is a crucial issue in our day. Many religious groups base doctrine on what they claim is revelation added to Scripture.

Claims for Continuing Revelation

Mormonism

The Church of Jesus Christ of Latter-day Saints claims that "the Book of Mormon is a volume of holy scripture comparable to the Bible."[22] Mormonism clearly asserts that the *Book of Mormon* is revelation that God added to His Word. This group's "Articles of Faith" also affirms a commitment to continuing revelation. The seventh statement reads, "We believe in the gift of tongues, prophecy, revelation, visions, healing, interpretation of tongues, and so forth."[23]

Seventh-day Adventism

The Seventh-day Adventists make a similar claim:

The church of the living God is "the pillar and foundation of the truth" (I Tim. 3:15, NIV). It is the depository and citadel of truth, protecting truth from the attacks of its enemies. Truth, however, is dynamic, not static. If members claim to have new light—a new doctrine or a new interpretation of the Scriptures—those of experience

---

[22]"Introduction, *The Book of Mormon* (Salt Lake City: Corporation of the President of the Church of Jesus Christ of Latter-day Saints, 1981), n.p.

[23]"The Articles of Faith of the Church of Jesus Christ of Latter-day Saints" (Salt Lake City: Corporation of the President of The Church of Jesus Christ of Latter-day Saints, 1988), one page.

should test the new teaching by the standard of Scripture (see Isa. 8:20). If the new light meets this standard, then the church must accept it; if not, it should reject it.[24]

This statement subtly makes the Seventh-day Adventist church the final authority in determining truth. This is how the Adventists justify Ellen G. White's writings as authoritative. Lest anyone think we are reading too much into this, note that the Adventists affirm that the gift of prophecy is active in the Church today.[25] In the middle of the same section they claim,

The gift of prophecy was active in the ministry of Ellen G. White, one of the founders of the Seventh-day Adventist Church. She has given *inspired instruction* for God's people living during the time of the end [emphasis mine].[26]

The Adventists try to "have their cake and eat it too." The chapter cited tries to set the Scriptures apart as unique, yet claims at the same time that Ellen G. White's writings are prophetic and inspired.

Roman Catholicism

The Roman Catholic Church adds tradition and the authority of the church to the Bible.

The most holy ecumenical and general Synod of Trent . . . following the example of the orthodox fathers . . . receives and venerates with equal devotion and reverence all the books both of the Old and New Testaments (since God is the author of both) and also said traditions, both those pertaining to faith and those pertaining to morals, as dictated either orally by Christ or by the Holy Spirit and preserved by continuous succession in the Catholic Church.[27]

---

[24]*Seventh-day Adventists Believe . . .* (Washington, DC: Ministerial Association, General Conference of Seventh-day Adventists, 1988), pp. 140-41.
[25]Ibid., pp. 219-29.
[26]Ibid., p. 224.
[27]Martin Chemnitz, *Examination of the Council of Trent*, Vol. I, translated by Fred

The Second Vatican Council stated without equivocation that the Word of God is qualified by tradition and the teaching of the church. We must cite three lengthy passages, for we need to see Rome's teaching clearly.

> But in order to keep the Gospel forever whole and alive within the Church, the Apostles left bishops as their successors, "handing over" to them "the authority to teach in their own place." This sacred tradition, therefore, *and Sacred Scripture* of both the Old and New Testaments are like a mirror in which the pilgrim Church on earth looks at God, from whom she has received everything, until she is brought finally to see Him as He is, face to face (see 1 John 3:2) [emphasis mine].[28]

The Vatican II statement makes a clear distinction between tradition and Scripture. It continues,

> Hence there exists a close connection and communication between sacred tradition and Sacred Scripture. For both of them, flowing from the same divine wellspring, in a certain way merge into a unity and tend toward the same end. . . . Consequently *it is not from sacred Scripture alone that the Church draws her certainty about everything which has been revealed. Therefore both sacred tradition and sacred Scripture are to be accepted and venerated with the same sense of loyalty and reverence* [emphasis mine].[29]

Vatican II leaves no question about the issue of her authority. Chapter II, "Handing on Divine Revelation," concludes with this statement:

> It is clear, therefore, that sacred tradition, Sacred Scripture and the teaching authority of the Church, in accord

---

Kramer (St. Louis: Concordia Publishing House, 1978), p. 37, Quoted in John E. Milheim, ed., *Let Rome Speak for Herself* (Schaumburg, IL: Regular Baptist Press, 1982), p. 18.

[28]*Dogmatic Constitution on Divine Revelation DEI VERBUM Solemnly Promulgated by His Holiness, Pope Paul VI on November 18, 1965* (Rome: Vatican Web Site, http://www.vatican.va), chapter II, 7.

[29]Ibid., chapter II, 9.

with God's most wise design, are so linked and joined together that one cannot stand without the others, and that all together and each in its own way under the action of the one Holy Spirit contribute effectively to the salvation of souls.[30]

Rome's position is that the Scriptures, tradition, and the teaching authority of the church combine to give God's revelation to men and provide for man's salvation. This is diametrically opposed to Jude's statement.

The Charismatics

Jack Deere represents the position of many, if not most, Charismatics today. His book, *Surprised by the Voice of God,* bears the subtitle "How God Speaks Today Through Prophecies, Dreams, and Visions."[31] Deere's contention is obviously that outside of His Word God speaks to men today. He advances the theory that God uses special revelation today and that the revelatory gifts have not ceased.

We do not mean to belittle those with whom we disagree; but the Charismatic position is untenable, and Deere makes claims that leave the thinking reader incredulous. Let him tell his own story and make his own claim:

> The other day I was running on a treadmill and listening through headphones to a portable CD player. I wish I could say it was Beethoven or Bach I was listening to. It wasn't even contemporary Christian music; it was plain ol' country western. A love song came on, and the *voice of God* came through the words of the ballad. How did I know it was God? Because a sharp, clean edge of conviction slit an opening in my heart. I had been insensitive and ungrateful to the woman I love. Leesa never said anything. Maybe she didn't notice it, or maybe she chose to

---

[30]Ibid., chapter II, 10.
[31]Jack Deere, *Surprised by the Voice of God: How God Speaks Today Through Prophecies, Dreams, and Visions* (Grand Rapids: Zondervan, 1996), p. 3.

ignore it. I was certainly oblivious to it—until the song came on. When it did, the lyrics laid bare my sin in such a specific way that it not only shamed me but humbled me to repent.

Still not sure it was God speaking to me? *Scripture says it was*, for the Holy Spirit is the only Person powerful enough to break through the darkness of the human heart with a conviction of sin which leads to repentance (John 16:8). If you're wondering of what particular sin I repented, keep wondering—I'm not telling. All I can tell you is this. *The words may have been from Nashville, but the message was from Heaven.* And it was a message for me. A message that moved me to bring my life in harmony not only with the Word of God . . . but also with my wife [emphasis mine].[32]

But Deere's claim overlooks the truth that God's revelation is sufficient for all the believer's needs. Paul tells us that the inspired Word "is profitable for doctrine, for reproof, for correction, for instruction in righteousness" (II Tim. 3:16). Peter states that God's power has "given unto us all things that pertain unto life and godliness" (II Pet. 1:3) and that these "things" are in the "exceeding great and precious promises" of Scripture (II Pet. 1:4). Deere's statement is a tacit statement that Scripture is not sufficient and that God was forced to turn to a worldly Nashville singer to accomplish what the Word of God could not do. That is an illogical and ridiculous conclusion.

Beyond this, does not the Scripture tell us that it does a convicting or reproving work (II Tim. 3:16) because it is a revelation from God? Therefore fresh revelation is not needed for each convicting work God does. It appears that Deere has confused conviction and revelation.

---

[32]Ibid., pp. 128-29.

Peter Ruckman

Peter Ruckman is the leader of a cult-like movement that popularly claims inspiration for the King James Version of the Bible. He advocates "the A.V. 1611 as the final authority 'in all matters of faith and practice.' "[33] The purpose here is not to examine or dispute Ruckman's approach to the debate over manuscripts and translations. Ruckman takes his position to an illogical conclusion in chapter 8 of his book, entitled "Correcting the Greek with the English." After dealing with eleven passages in the New Testament that reflect textual variations in the manuscripts or problem translations (e.g., "robbers of churches" rather than "robbers of temples" in Acts 19:37),[34] Ruckman comes to this astounding conclusion: "Moral: 'Mistakes in the A.V. 1611 are advanced revelation!' " [emphasis Ruckman's].[35] The conclusion is obvious that in his zeal to defend a particular approach to the text of Scripture, and particularly a certain English version of the Bible, Ruckman has fallen into the trap of which Warfield warned. He has actually adopted "the second of the lowered views of inspiration" in which he has subjected the Scriptures to his own supposedly "enlightened reason."[36] Thus he advocates an advanced revelation beyond what God spoke through the writers of the Scripture.

Approach to a Completed Revelation

Up to this point we have cited just two passages of Scripture to support the contention that the Bible is a completed revelation. Jude's statement is forceful (Jude 3). John's warning

---

[33]Peter S. Ruckman, *The Christian's Handbook of Manuscript Evidence* (Pensacola, FL: Pensacola Bible Press, 1970), p. 7.

[34]Ibid., pp. 125-26.

[35]Ibid., p. 126.

[36]Warfield, p. 113.

at the end of the Revelation *and* at the end of the canon of Scripture seems emphatic. Yet is there more? Can we really make a case for the position that God is not speaking to men today as He did when He gave His Word? When a cacophony of voices contends, for one reason or another, that God still reveals Himself, we must deal with this question. Christians deserve a certain, biblical, and reasonable explanation of the biblical teaching on this subject.

Little Written

One is amazed at how little is written affirming that Scripture is a completed unit of revelation. Perhaps the older writers, thoroughly combating the rationalistic attacks on Scripture, did not see the need to contend against the mystical attacks on it. Most of the classic systematic theologies or works on the inspiration of Scripture contain a brief statement about the issue.[37] Pache is typical when he says, "All the revelations discussed above were accorded to individuals or to generations now passed away."[38] Certainly the Pentecostal and now Charismatic movement was not as prevalent as it is today. To be sure, Baptist theologians have affirmed that Scripture is the sole authority for faith and practice. They have argued against Rome's threefold authority structure of Scripture, tradition, and church authority. But we can find almost nothing that explains *why* Scripture is complete or *how* we know that it is.

John MacArthur has written probably the best current book on the Charismatic movement. He deals with this issue

---

[37]F. David Farnell has written four articles in *Bibliotheca Sacra* and one in *The Master's Theological Journal*. Farnell is a cessationist, holding that we do not receive continuing revelation today. The articles are in response to Wayne Grudem's views to the opposite. We will cite some of Farnell's writing, but it is highly technical and not for the popular reader.

[38]Pache, p. 23.

clearly but briefly.[39] Peter Masters has a chapter entitled "Proving the Gifts Have Ceased" in which he deals with the cessation of all sign gifts, including prophecy.[40] His work is also helpful.

Approaching the Issue

We confront an apparent problem when dealing with the issue of a completed revelation versus continuing revelation. Scripture is clear that God revealed Himself progressively as He gave the Scripture. Hebrews 1:1, 2 explain that "God, who at sundry times and in divers manners spake in time past unto the fathers by the prophets, Hath in these last days spoken unto us by his Son." We have previously noted the major ways by which God made His revelation to men.

Both the Old and New Testaments give clear instruction for discerning false prophets. The New Testament teaches that God gave signs and wonders to vindicate apostolic revelation. Scripture also teaches that God will again give supernatural revelation with miracles vindicating it (Joel 2:28). This will occur during the Tribulation. Rolland McCune affirms that "As a matter of fact, the rapture initiates a whole new era of revelation; there will be widespread revelatory activity during the Tribulation and Millennium (Rev. 11:3; Joel 2:28).[41]

As we approach this issue, we must answer this question: If there *was* supernatural revelation during the time God gave the Scriptures, and if *there will be* supernatural revelation during the time of the Tribulation, *how do we know we are not receiving revelation today?*

---

[39]John F. MacArthur, Jr., *Charismatic Chaos* (Grand Rapids: Zondervan Publishing House, 1992), pp. 60-65.

[40]Peter Masters, *The Healing Epidemic* (London: The Wakeman Trust, 1988), pp. 112-35.

[41]Rolland D. McCune, "A Biblical Study of Tongues and Miracles" (Minneapolis: Central Baptist Theological Seminary, n.d.), p. 8.

Evidence for a Completed Revelation

Since God gave revelation to those who lived during Bible times and since He will give revelation again during the Tribulation, it is possible to discover God's approach to this subject. Understanding God's guidelines for distinguishing true revelation from false will enable us to biblically evaluate the claims of those who say that God has revealed Himself to them. In this section we will examine three Old Testament passages and three in the New Testament that inform our thinking on this subject.

Deuteronomy 13:1-5—The Theological Test

If there arise among you a prophet, or a dreamer of dreams, and giveth thee a sign or a wonder, And the sign or the wonder come to pass, whereof he spake unto thee, saying, Let us go after other gods, which thou hast not known, and let us serve them; Thou shalt not hearken unto the words of that prophet, or that dreamer of dreams: for the Lord your God proveth you, to know whether ye love the Lord your God with all your heart and with all your soul. Ye shall walk after the Lord your God, and fear him, and keep his commandments, and obey his voice, and ye shall serve him, and cleave unto him. And that prophet, or that dreamer of dreams, shall be put to death; because he hath spoken to turn you away from the Lord your God, which brought you out of the land of Egypt, and redeemed you out of the house of bondage, to thrust thee out of the way which the Lord thy God commanded thee to walk in. So shalt thou put the evil away from the midst of thee.

God warns Israel against a prophet who may arise among them. This prophet will come with a purported revelation received by prophecy or dream (v. 1). He will support his prophecy with a miracle. The miracle, according to verse two, may actually come to pass. The purpose of the prophet's message is to seduce Israel to serve other gods: "Let us go after other gods, which thou hast not known, and let us serve them" (v. 2). Notice that according to verse three, the nation is to reject the prophet, even though he gives a claimed revelation and accredits it with a miracle! Part of God's purpose in allowing this seducer to come is to prove His people's love for Him (v. 3).[42] The sensational and miraculous is *not* the sole vindication and authentication of a purported revelation.

Criteria for Judging Prophetic Claims

In verse four God describes the standard by which all claimed prophecy must be judged. All supposed prophecy, to be genuine, must be consistent with (1) the character of God ("Ye shall walk after the Lord your God") and (2) the already written Word of God ("His commandments, His voice"). These claims to additional revelation must also result in (3) the fear of God ("fear Him"), (4) obedience to God ("obey His voice"), and (5) devotion to Him ("and cleave unto Him"). Any prophetic claim to genuineness must be consistent with what we know about the character of God as it is revealed in His Word. It must also promote obedience to and love for God. Any prophetic claim that does not "square" with the character of God and His revealed Word exposes itself as patently false.

Source of False Prophecy

Several times Scripture indicates that Satan's activity motivates false prophecy. Deuteronomy 13:12, 13 seem to teach this fact. Passages like Matthew 24:24; II Thessalonians 2:9; Revelation 13:11-14; 16:14; and 19:20 also support this idea. In fact, it seems that the false prophet of Revelation 13, who will appear during the Great Tribulation, perfectly fits the model of Deuteronomy 13:1-5.

---

[42]Our first and greatest duty to God is to love Him. See Deuteronomy 6:1-7; 10:12, 13; 30:6; Matthew 22:37; Mark 12:29, 30; Luke 10:27.

Modern Prophecy Exposed

This biblical standard exposes current claims to prophecy as clearly false. We could cite many examples here, but one will suffice. Notice a statement by the popular Charismatic preacher Kenneth Copeland. He says:

> It's time for these things to happen, saith the Lord. It's time for spiritual activity to increase. Oh, yes, demonic activity will increase along at the same time. But don't let that disturb you. Don't be disturbed when people accuse you of thinking you're God. Don't be disturbed when people accuse you of a fanatical way of life. Don't be disturbed when people put you down and speak harshly and roughly of you. They spoke that way of Me, should they not speak that way of you? The more you get to be like Me, the more they're going to think that way of you. *They crucified me for claiming that I was God. But I didn't claim I was God; I just claimed I walked with Him and that He was in Me. Hallelujah. That's what you're doing"* [emphasis mine].[43]

Please note that Copeland is guilty of heresy on two counts. First, he says that Jesus did not claim to be God. That statement is false when judged by the standard of John 5:18; 10:30; and 14:7, 9. Copeland robs Jesus of His deity. Second, Copeland elevates man to the level of Christ. We are, according to Copeland, making the same claims that Christ made. The author of Hebrews tells us that Jesus was made like men in His humanity (Heb. 2:14-17). He also sets Christ apart as unique and different from men in His deity (Heb. 7:26). In two sentences Copeland diminishes the deity of Christ and promotes an exaltation of man. Both statements radically differ from revealed Scripture. This twentieth-century prophet does not meet the biblical standard and must be rejected.

---

[43] Kenneth Copeland, *Believer's Voice of Victory*, February 1987, quoted in MacArthur, p. 57.

Deuteronomy 18:15-22—The Practical Test

The Lord thy God will raise up unto thee a Prophet from the midst of thee, of thy brethren, like unto me; unto him ye shall hearken; According to all that thou desiredst of the Lord thy God in Horeb in the day of the assembly, saying, Let me not hear again the voice of the Lord my God, neither let me see this great fire any more, that I die not. And the Lord said unto me, They have well spoken that which they have spoken. I will raise them up a Prophet from among their brethren, like unto thee, and will put my words in his mouth; and he shall speak unto them all that I shall command him. And it shall come to pass, that whosoever will not hearken unto my words which he shall speak in my name, I will require it of him. But the prophet, which shall presume to speak a word in my name, which I have not commanded him to speak, or that shall speak in the name of other gods, even that prophet shall die. And if thou say in thine heart, How shall we know the word which the Lord hath not spoken? When a prophet speaketh in the name of the Lord, if the thing follow not, nor come to pass, that is the thing which the Lord hath not spoken, but the prophet hath spoken it presumptuously; thou shalt not be afraid of him.

A Messianic Prophecy

Any consideration of this passage must begin by acknowledging that this prophecy is fulfilled in Jesus Christ. Philip told his brother Nathanael "We have found him, of whom Moses in the law, and the prophets, did write, Jesus of Nazareth, the son of Joseph" (John 1:45). Peter directly quoted Deuteronomy 18:15, 18, affirming that Jesus fulfilled the prophecy (Acts 3:20-22).

A Consistent Prophecy

This statement is consistent with the previous statement of Deuteronomy 13:1-5. Verse twenty teaches us, "But the prophet, which shall presume to speak a word in my name, which I have not commanded him to speak, or that shall speak in the name of other gods, even that prophet shall die." This statement is consistent with the criteria and the warning given in Deuteronomy 13:4, 5. So this passage builds on the theological standard set in the previous passage.

A Credible Prophecy

> And if thou say in thine heart, How shall we know the word which the Lord hath not spoken? When a prophet speaketh in the name of the Lord, if the thing follow not, nor come to pass, that is the thing which the Lord hath not spoken, but the prophet hath spoken it presumptuously; thou shalt not be afraid of him (Deut. 18:21-22).

God's practical test for the prophet is that his prophecy must come true. God requires the prophet to speak with total accuracy. In later years God's judgment came on the nation of Israel. One of the causes for God's judgment was that "her prophets have daubed them with untempered mortar, seeing vanity and divining lies unto them, saying, Thus saith the Lord God, when the Lord hath not spoken" (Ezek. 20:28). God judged the nation and her lying prophets. God's men spoke, by divine requirement, with complete accuracy.

A Contested Prophecy

The Charismatics recognize that this passage destroys their claims to authentic prophecy. They labor mightily against its teaching in three ways. First, they argue that the Old Testament strictures do not apply to New Testament prophecy. They claim two forms of prophecy in the New Testament, apostolic and non-apostolic. They contend that New Testament apostles spoke inspired words. They further argue that New Testament prophets who were not apostles were not inspired in the same ways as the apostles or Old Testament prophets. Wayne Grudem writes,

Much more commonly, prophet and prophecy were used of ordinary Christians who spoke not with absolute divine authority, but simply to report something God had laid on their hearts or brought to their minds. There are many indications in the New Testament that this ordinary gift of prophecy had authority less than that of the Bible, and even less than that of recognized Bible teaching in the early church.[44]

Farnell further quotes Grudem: "Only NT apostles spoke inspired words. The very words of NT prophets were not inspired as were those of OT prophets."[45]

Second, the Charismatics simply assert that some prophecy may be erroneous. Deere states,

Some people think one missed or failed prediction makes a person a false prophet. The Bible, though, doesn't call someone a false prophet for simply missing a prediction. In the Scripture, false prophets are those who *contradict* the teaching and predictions of true prophets and attempt to lead people away from God and his Word [emphasis Deere's].[46]

The biblical response to Deere's statement is a "bad news, good news" statement. The "bad news" is that Deere's first assertion is simply wrong. Deuteronomy 18:22 clearly discredits the prophet because he "missed the prediction," as Deere says. The language of Ezekiel 13:1-9 and 22:28 is unmistakable. The false prophets were false because they spoke lies. Argue as he will, Deere cannot escape the requirement that the prophecy must come true. The "good news" in Deere's statement is that the last half of it is correct. False prophets may also seek to lead people astray after another god (Deut. 13:2).

---

[44]Wayne A. Grudem, "Still Prophesy," 30, quoted in F. David Farnell, "Fallible New Testament Prophecy/Prophets? A Critique of Wayne Grudem's Hypothesis," *The Master's Seminary Journal*, n.d., p. 161.

[45]Ibid.

[46]Deere, p. 68.

Third, Charismatics argue for a difference between Old Testament and New Testament prophecy. They further contend that New Testament prophecy is not held to the same standard of one hundred percent accuracy as Old Testament prophecy. Grudem states his position succinctly:

> On the other side, I am asking those in the cessationist camp to give serious thought to the possibility that prophecy in ordinary New Testament churches was not equal to Scripture in authority, but was simply a very human—and sometimes partially mistaken—report of something the Holy Spirit brought to someone's mind.[47]

Farnell explains the ramifications of Grudem's position:

> This leaves Grudem with two forms of New Testament prophecy: nonauthoritative "congregational" prophecy and authoritative (i.e., apostolic) prophecy. The crucial point of his thesis is that apostles, not New Testament prophets, were the true successors of the Old Testament prophets and spoke like their earlier counterparts with the authority derived from the inspiration of their words.[48]

It appears that the only way to justify the Charismatic type of prophecy that occurs today is to establish a difference between the prophetic gifts of the Old and New Testaments. This simply cannot be done.

First, the standard of perfection (Deut. 18:20, 21) appears in the context of a Messianic prophecy. The standard requiring one hundred percent accuracy applied to Christ in an era after Old Testament prophecy ceased. If one portion of that passage is valid in the New Testament era, then the rest of it must apply too. The requirement that the prophet speak with

---

[47]Wayne Grudem, *The Gift of Prophecy in the New Testament and Today* (Westchester, IL: Crossway Books, 1988), pp. 14-15, quoted in F. David Farnell, "The Current Debate about New Testament Prophecy," *Bibliotheca Sacra,* July-September 1992, p. 280.

[48]Farnell, "The Current Debate," p. 281.

one hundred percent accuracy must apply to the New Testament prophet also.

New Testament prophecy rests on Old Testament prophecy. Farnell argues for a *continuity* between Old Testament and New Testament prophecy. He makes several arguments. They include (1) the continuity between Joel 2:28-32 and Acts 2:17-21, (2) the continuity between the Old and New Testament prophets (Mal. 3:1; 4:4-6; with Matt. 3:3-17; Mark 1:3-8; Luke 3:4-17; Matt. 11:9-11), (3) the similarity between Agabus and the Old Testament prophets (Acts 21:11), (4) the continuity of John the Apostle with Old Testament Prophets (Rev. 22:7-9), (5) the similarity of language used by prophets in both Testaments, (6) the warnings about false prophets in both Testaments (Deut. 13, 18; Matt. 24:11), and (7) the fact that prophets were empowered by the Spirit of God in both Testaments.[49]

Joel 2:28-32

> And it shall come to pass afterward, that I will pour out my spirit upon all flesh; and your sons and your daughters shall prophesy, your old men shall dream dreams, your young men shall see visions: And also upon the servants and upon the handmaids in those days will I pour out my spirit. And I will show wonders in the heavens and in the earth, blood, and fire, and pillars of smoke. The sun shall be turned into darkness, and the moon into blood before the great and terrible day of the Lord come.

Joel 2:28 gives its own rules and guidelines for its fulfillment. Most believers acknowledge that this prophecy was partially fulfilled at Pentecost (Acts 2:16). However, Charles L. Feinberg takes a somewhat different position:

---

[49]F. David Farnell, "The Gift of Prophecy in the Old and New Testaments," *Bibliotheca Sacra*, October-December 1992, pp. 39-405. Farnell has done excellent and extremely detailed work in these articles. The reader may wish to consult the entire series in *Bibliotheca Sacra*.

Peter distinctly states that he is referring to the prediction of Joel. However, that fact alone does not constitute a fulfillment. In the first place, the customary formula for a fulfilled prophecy is entirely lacking in Acts 2:16. And even more telling is the fact that much of Joel's prophecy, even as quoted in Acts 2:19-20, was not fulfilled at that time. We cannot take the position that only a portion of the prophecy was meant to be fulfilled at all, because this would work havoc with Bible prophecy. God predicts and He can perform just what He predicted. The best position to take is that Peter used Joel's prophecy as an illustration of what was transpiring in his day and not as a fulfillment of this prediction. In short, Peter saw in the events of his day proof that God would yet completely bring to pass all that Joel prophesied. Joel's prophecy, then was prefilled; it is yet (as the Old Testament passages on the outpouring of the Spirit show) to be fulfilled.[50]

This seems to stretch the point. The Scriptures contain many prophecies with dual fulfillment. Abraham's prophecy in Genesis 22:8 was fulfilled in 22:13 and in John 1:29. Isaiah's prophecy of 7:13-16 was fulfilled in 8:1-4 and more completely in Matthew 1:22, 23. It seems better to agree that the prophecy of Joel was partially fulfilled at Pentecost and will be completely fulfilled during the Tribulation and the Millennium to follow. The statements of Matthew 24:29, 30; Mark 13:24, 25; Luke 21:11, 25; and Revelation 6:12 indicate that the passage has a future prophetic fulfillment during the Tribulation period.

Charismatic Assertion

The Charismatics draw the faulty conclusion that the Charismatic manifestations are fulfillment of this prophecy. Speaking of Pentecost, Deere states,

---

[50]Charles L. Feinberg, *The Minor Prophets* (Chicago: Moody Press, 1980), pp. 81-82.

Peter claimed that the day of Pentecost was the beginning of the fulfillment of Joel 2:28-32. . . . With the coming of the Spirit there is a sense in which every Christian is to be prophetic. There will be prophecies, dreams, and visions in the church without distinction in regard to gender, age, or economic position.[51]

The Biblical Evidence

Deere's conclusion is faulty. Joel prophesied that the supernatural gifts of the Spirit (prophecy, dreams, and visions, v. 28) would be accompanied by divine supernatural manifestations in the physical world (blood, fire, smoke, the sun darkened, the moon turned to blood, vv. 30, 32). In other words, God's supernatural work in the earth will accompany and vindicate the supernatural manifestation of the Spirit in God's people. This pattern was fulfilled at Pentecost. The wind and fire accompanied the gift of tongues (Acts 2:1-4). These divine manifestations in nature will also mark the prophetic occurrences of which Christ spoke and John prophesied. See Matthew 24:29, 30; Mark 13:24, 25; Luke 21:11, 25; and Revelation 6:12.

We conclude that if there is to be a valid fulfillment of Joel 2:28-32 today, it must combine the element of supernatural phenomena in the physical realm with the supernatural manifestation of the gifts of the Spirit. The modern Charismatic movement cannot demonstrate both these elements.

1 Corinthians 13:8-10

Charity never faileth: but whether there be prophecies, they shall fail; whether there be tongues, they shall cease; whether there be knowledge, it shall vanish away. For we

---

[51]Deere, p. 179. Earlier, on page 101, he makes a similar statement: "When the Holy Spirit brought the mighty wind and the tongues of fire on the Day of Pentecost, many thought the 120 people from the Upper Room were drunk. But God opened Peter's mind to understand that these phenomena were the *beginning* of a fulfillment of the ancient prophecy spoken of in Joel 2:28-32" [emphasis mine].

know in part, and we prophesy in part. But when that which is perfect is come, then that which is in part shall be done away.

Vehicles of Progressive Revelation

These verses deal with three separate spiritual gifts—prophecies, tongues, and knowledge. Prophecy is clearly a gift through which God gave special revelation to men (Heb. 1:1, 2; Eph. 3:5). The gift of knowledge was likely a channel for revelation also.[52] Paul states flatly that all three of the gifts will end (v. 8). He teaches that these gifts are "in part" (v. 9). They are some of the means God used to give partial and progressive revelation. Further, Paul specifies the time when these gifts would cease. He says, "But when that which is perfect is come, then that which is in part shall be done away" (v. 10).

A Completed Revelation

In contrast to gifts that are "in part" (v. 9), Paul speaks in verse ten of "that which is perfect." The meaning of "that which is perfect" is variously understood. Deere uses the term three times to refer to the partial knowledge of the prophet, whether present-day or apostolic.[53] This does not seem to square with Paul's statement that the prophecy itself was partial and stood in contrast to an anticipated complete revelation. Tongues advocates generally use the term in reference to the rapture of the church.[54] McCune points out that this is not reasonable because the terms that refer to the rapture

---

[52]Lester L. Lippincott III, "A Study of 'That Which Is Perfect' in First Corinthians 13:10" (Th.M. thesis, Detroit Baptist Theological Seminary, 1990), pp. 37-42, gives a concise analysis of the varying views of the gift of knowledge. He assembles convincing argumentation that it was a supernatural gift through which God gave special revelation. The account of Peter dealing with Ananias and Sapphira (Acts 5:1-11) is a case in point.

[53]Deere, pp. 155, 245, 330.

[54]McCune, p. 9.

(*parousia*, *epiphaneia*, and *apokalupsis*) are feminine terms, while "perfect" is a neuter word. We have also previously noted[55] that with the rapture, God will begin a whole new era of revelation. He further notes that "perfect" cannot refer to Christ since it is a neuter term, and a reference to Christ Himself "would be masculine."[56] He comes to a forceful conclusion:

> Since "that which is perfect" is in intended contrast with the partial or incomplete revelatory process (cf. 1 Cor. 13:10 with v. 9), and since it is the cause of the doing away of that which is "in part" (1 Cor. 13:10) the "completed thing" most naturally would refer to the completed process of revelation in the first century which is embodied in the New Testament canon.[57]

Prophecy was a God-ordained method by which God gave partial revelation to men in a progressive order. God stated that it would come to an end when His revelation was completed. With the completion of Scripture, we should look for no more revelation in this age. We have God's completed Word.

Hebrews 1:1, 2

> God, who at sundry times and in divers manners spake in time past unto the fathers by the prophets, Hath in these last days spoken unto us by his Son, whom he hath appointed heir of all things, by whom also he made the worlds.

We have already noted that these verses speak of God's continuing revelation through the prophets. These two verses also point to the finality of God's revelation in Christ.[58] Jesus

---

[55]See p. 47.
[56]McCune, p. 9.
[57]Ibid.
[58]R.C.H. Lenski, *The Interpretation of the Epistle to the Hebrews and the Epistle of James* (Minneapolis: Augsburg Publishing House, 1966), p. 31, points this out. The

Christ is the culmination of God's revelation. He is the fulfillment of God's promises throughout the Old Testament. "The consummation of the revelatory process, the definitive revelation, took place when . . . the very Son of God came."[59] With Him, and what the apostles wrote about Him, God's revelation is complete. Lenski explains this further:

> This means that now, having spoken in the person of his Son, we have the ultimate Word and revelation of God. No more and nothing further will God ever say to men. They who look for more revelation will never find it; [Heb.] 2:3 is God's answer to them; likewise Deut. 18:19. This is certain also because the Old Testament promises of redemption have been fulfilled by the incarnate Son.[60]

Hebrews 2:1-4

> Therefore we ought to give the more earnest heed to the things which we have heard, lest at any time we should let them slip. For if the word spoken by angels was stedfast, and every transgression and disobedience received a just recompense of reward; how shall we escape, if we neglect so great salvation; which at the first began to be spoken by the Lord, and was confirmed unto us by them that heard him; God also bearing them witness, both with signs and wonders, and with divers miracles, and gifts of the Holy Ghost, according to his own will?

This New Testament passage indicates that God verified His New Testament revelation with signs and wonders. It further teaches that both the revelation and the accrediting signs and wonders have ceased.

---

author of Hebrews uses the word "λαλέω"—"to speak"—twice. The first time, the Holy Spirit inspires him to use an aorist participle, "having spoken," which looks forward to the main aorist verb, "he spoke." Lenski calls this an "aorist of finality."

[59]Leon Morris, "Hebrews" in Frank E. Gaebelein, ed., *The Expositor's Bible Commentary* (Grand Rapids: Zondervan Publishing House, 1981), 12:13.

[60]Lenski, p. 33.

Comparison to Old Testament Revelation
The term "the word spoken by angels" (v. 2) appears to be a reference to the Old Testament revelation. Stephen (Acts 7:35, 53) and Paul (Gal. 3:19) speak of the ministry of angels in communicating God's Old Testament revelation. An angel met Moses at the burning bush. We are not certain just what the function of angels was in the giving of the Law. Lenski surmises that God may have used angels to cause "the thunders, the lightnings, the terrible trumpetings."[61]

Scripture tells us the Law was "steadfast." The word *bebaioo* (v. 2) means "standing firm on the feet, steadfast, maintaining firmness or solidity."[62] God has confirmed His Word, or shown it to be valid. In both the Greek and Jewish worlds, the word was used of a legally binding agreement a seller would give to a buyer in the presence of a third party.[63] God established His Old Testament revelation to men. It is His Word, His bond, valid and binding. It stood in condemnation of every disobedience (v. 2).

The New Testament Revelation
The New Testament revelation "at first began to be spoken by the Lord, and was confirmed unto us by them that heard him" (v. 3). God's work of revelation ceased with the completion of the Old Testament and did not begin again until Christ resumed it. "Jesus was God's full revelation and he is the source of this new and superior revelation."[64] This passage clearly shows us the instruments through which the New Testament revelation came. It was "spoken by the Lord, and was confirmed unto us by them that heard him" (v. 3).

[61]Lenski, p. 65.
[62]Heinrich Schlier, "βεβαιόω" in Gerhard Kittle, ed., *Theological Dictionary of the New Testament* (Grand Rapids: Wm. B. Eerdmans Publishing Co., 1964), I:601.
[63]Ibid., I:602.
[64]A. T. Robertson, *Word Pictures in the New Testament* (Grand Rapids: Baker Book House, 1932), V:343.

Those who heard the Lord Jesus were the apostles. Christ and the apostles were the ones chosen by God to give this revelation to men. This rules out further revelation after the time of the apostles.

Just as the Old Testament revelation was steadfast (v. 2), the New Testament revelation was confirmed (v. 3). The same word translated "stedfast" in verse two is translated "confirmed" in verse three. Both Testaments are God's fixed revelation. He stands by one as surely as He does the other. Note the continuity and similarity between Old Testament and New Testament revelation.

God's Witness to His Revelation

God gave witness to Christ and the apostles as they preached and wrote. He testified to the authenticity of their ministries and messages with signs, wonders, and various miracles. Thus, signs and wonders accredited the messengers of the New Testament revelation. The word "bearing them witness" (v. 4) is important. It is the word *sunepimartureo*. Its root is *martureo*, which means "to bear witness." This compound form of the word is used only here in the New Testament. The idea of the word is that God bore witness, by means of the signs and wonders, along with other witnesses, giving additional testimony.[65] Arndt and Gingrich give the basic definition of the word as "testify at the same time."[66]

Conclusions

The facts of this passage bring us to some inescapable conclusions. God revealed Himself through Christ and those who heard Him, that is, the apostles. God confirmed and established His Word to men in the New Testament just as

---

[65]M. R. Vincent, *Word Studies in the New Testament* (1887; reprint, Grand Rapids: Wm. B. Eerdmans Publishing Company, 1989), IV: 396.

[66]Arndt and Gingrich, p. 795.

He did with the Old Testament. As Christ and the apostles preached, taught, and wrote, God bore witness to their ministries with the additional evidence of signs, wonders, miracles, and gifts of the Holy Spirit. The word "bearing witness" expresses the idea of "bearing witness at the same time." That means that the revelation from God and the supernatural evidences of it accompanied each other and were simultaneous with each other. The miracles accredited the revelation. God limited the means by which He made His revelation known. He revealed Himself only through Christ and the apostles. When God completed His work of revelation, the supernatural signs ceased. Paul understood the scope of his ministry and that the miracles he performed were tied to his office. He told the Corinthians, "Truly the signs of an apostle were wrought among you in all patience, in signs, and wonders, and mighty deeds" (II Cor. 12:12). We are receiving no more revelation from God in this age because we have no apostles. For this reason we should expect no miracles today. This passage "slams the door" on any idea of a valid, biblically justified revelation from God in this age.

Conclusion

Old Testament Passages

At least three Old Testament passages teach us about God's mind and purpose in His process of revelation. Deuteronomy 13:1-5 states that any valid prophecy will be consistent with that which has already been revealed in Scripture and the person and character of God as revealed to us in Scripture.

Deuteronomy 18:15-18 teaches that the true prophet speaks with total accuracy. We must regard all who claim to be prophets and do not meet this standard as false. In the Old

Testament theocracy such false prophets would have been stoned to death!

Scripture demonstrates a continuity between Old Testament and New Testament prophecy. The same theological test for Old Testament prophets applies to New Testament prophets. The same practical test for Old Testament prophets applies to New Testament prophets. The Deuteronomy passages lead us to the conclusion that no current claims to prophecy from God are valid.

Joel 2:28 teaches, and Acts 2:17-21 confirms, that the Holy Spirit's supernatural gift of prophecy will be accompanied by God's supernatural manifestations in the physical universe. At the very least, Joel 2:28-32 destroys the validity of any current, supposedly revelatory gift of the Spirit.

New Testament Passages

We conclude that revelation has ceased. I Corinthians 13:8-10 teaches that God gave partial revelation through prophecy. With the completed revelation, the partial revelations ceased. Hebrews 1:1, 2 declare that Jesus Christ is the culmination of God's revelation. Hebrews 2:1-4 affirms that New Testament revelation came through Christ and the apostles. It ended when their respective ministries were completed. We conclude that signs and wonders have ceased because God sovereignly gave them to accredit Christ and the apostles, who were the messengers of the New Testament revelation.

Certain statements seem to indicate that Scripture is a closed body of revelation. Jude 3 speaks of "the faith which was once delivered unto the saints." That forceful statement is convincing in itself and consistent with the teaching of Hebrews 2:1-4. The warning to those who would add to or take away from the Word of God, coming at the end of the Book of the Revelation (Rev. 22:18, 19) and at the end of the canon of Scripture, gives support to the same conclusions.

Here We Stand

This great affirmation that God has once for all, in a complete fashion, revealed truth to men is the foundation upon which Jude builds his description of New Testament Christianity. Since the Garden of Eden, Satan has attacked that Word of God. First-century believers were called upon to "earnestly contend for the faith" (Jude 3). In the late nineteenth and early twentieth centuries men again rose up to "do battle royal" for the same faith. We know that movement as Fundamentalism. It is not coincidence that this movement, in obedience to Jude's command, stands on the firm foundation that God laid in His excellent Word.

One of the early leaders in the twentieth-century Fundamentalist movement expressed the issue then and now in unequivocal terms. William Bell Riley said,

> In the last analysis, it comes wholly to one question. . . . Is the *book* we call the Bible divinely and infallibly inspired, a God-given revelation, or is it a purely human product, revealing the mental development of man in the process of evolution? [emphasis Riley's].[67]

With Paul, "I believe God" (Acts 27:25).

---

[67]William Bell Riley, "What Are the Real Questions Before the Northern Baptist Convention?" *Baptist*, June 18, 1921, quoted in Grant Wacker, *Augustus H. Strong and the Dilemma of Historical Consciousness* (Macon, GA: Mercer University Press, 1985), p. 117.

THE FUNDAMENTALISTS' FOUNDATION

Part II

How precious is the book divine,
By inspiration given!
Bright as a lamp its precepts shine,
To guide our souls to heaven.[1]

Beloved, when I gave all diligence to write unto you of the common salvation, it was needful for me to write unto you, and exhort you that ye should earnestly contend for the faith which was once delivered unto the saints (Jude 3).

The truth that believers possess a supernatural book from God is the foundation of New Testament Christianity. With this great truth, Jude begins the treatise in which he expounds on the essence of first-century Christianity and in which he exposes the character and error of the gospel's enemies. No wonder then, when propounding orthodox Christianity and standing against modernism's infiltration, that the early Fundamentalists saw the issue the same way. They articulated the biblical doctrine of the Scriptures and opposed those who denied the supernatural character of the Bible.

In 1919 leading orthodox Bible believers from several denominations organized the World Conference on Christian Fundamentals. These Christians, whom just one year later Curtis Lee Laws would call "Fundamentalists," met in Philadelphia. Joseph Kyle, a Lutheran leader and president of

---

[1]John Fawcett, "How Precious Is the Book Divine" in *Hymns of the Christian Life* (Camp Hill, PA: Christian Publications, Inc., 1976), p. 40.

Xenia Theological Seminary, preached on "The Word of God—the Foundation of the Fundamentals." In that stirring message, Kyle called the doctrine of Scripture "The Fundamental of Fundamentals."[2]

Jude's statement concerning the Scriptures teaches us that we have a body of truth that God *revealed* to the human race. The work of revelation, or "the divine act of communicating to man truth which otherwise man could not know,"[3] is the first element in the process God used to give us His Word. Several other biblical terms and ideas combine with revelation to make a complete doctrine of the Scriptures. The Bible teaches that God's Spirit moved on the authors of the Scripture so that it is *inspired*. We believe God has also *preserved* His Word. Jesus promised that the Holy Spirit would teach the Christian who studies the Word. We call that work of the Spirit *illumination*.

Since this doctrine is so critical to genuine Christianity, we propose in this chapter to briefly rehearse "those things which are most surely believed among us" (Luke 1:1). We will look at the biblical teaching on *inspiration*, *preservation*, and *illumination*. It is important to note what Luke says the reason is that these things came to be believed. In verse two Luke tells us that the "eyewitnesses, and ministers of the word" "delivered" them to us. The word "delivered" is the same word Jude uses to identify the Bible as revelation from God. Luke affirms that the apostles were the instruments of God's revelation. He builds on the same foundation of divine revelation as Jude.

─────────────────

[2]Joseph Kyle, "The Word of God—The Foundation of the Fundamentals" in *God Hath Spoken: Twenty-five Addresses Delivered at the World Conference of Christian Fundamentals* (Philadelphia: Bible Conference Committee, 1919), p. 65.

[3]Merrill F. Unger, *Introductory Guide to the Old Testament* (Grand Rapids: Zondervan Publishing House, 1956), p. 22.

Inspiration

Scripture teaches that God gave His Word by inspiration. Paul states,

> All scripture is given by inspiration of God, and is profitable for doctrine, for reproof, for correction, for instruction in righteousness: That the man of God may be perfect, throughly furnished unto all good works (II Tim. 3:16, 17).

Peter declares that God's Spirit was the agent of the work Paul calls inspiration. He tells us,

> Of which salvation the prophets have inquired and searched diligently, who prophesied of the grace that should come unto you: Searching what, or what manner of time the Spirit of Christ which was in them did signify, when it testified beforehand the sufferings of Christ, and the glory that should follow (I Pet. 1:10, 11).

He gives further light on the way God gave His Word when he says,

> We have also a more sure word of prophecy; whereunto ye do well that ye take heed, as unto a light that shineth in a dark place, until the day dawn, and the day star arise in your hearts: Knowing this first, that no prophecy of the scripture is of any private interpretation. For the prophecy came not in old time by the will of man: but holy men of God spake as they were moved by the Holy Ghost (II Pet. 1:19-21).

Inspiration Explained

A study of the subject of inspiration reveals many definitions of the term. When men believe the verbal, plenary inspiration of the Scriptures, their definitions will often parallel one another. Theologians have devoted entire volumes to the doctrine of the Bible. Our purpose here is to briefly survey and review this doctrine. Therefore, two definitions will be sufficient for our purposes.

René Pache states,

> Inspiration (in the limited sense of the word, as used in this work) is the determining influence exercised by the Holy Spirit on the writers of the Old and New Testaments in order that they might proclaim and set down in an exact and authentic way the message as received from God [emphasis Pache's].[4]

Warren Vanhetloo explains,

> Verbal plenary inspiration may be defined as that work of the Holy Spirit whereby the third person of the Trinity controlled and guided reception and communication of the divine message to mankind such that the word product is inerrantly authoritative.[5]

God-Breathed

The biblical word "inspiration" is the Greek word *theopneustos*. B. B. Warfield describes the importance of the word as the Holy Spirit prompted Paul to use it:

> What it says of Scripture is, not that it is "breathed into by God" or is the product of the divine "inbreathing" into its human authors, but that it is breathed out by God, "God breathed," the product of the creative breath of God.[6]

We can understand this in two ways. First, the "breath of God" in Scripture is a symbol of God's power. Psalm 33:6 speaks of the power of God's breath in creation. Isaiah 30:28, 33 associate the powerful breath of God with His judgment. We should remember that in the upper room the resurrected Jesus breathed on His disciples before instructing them, "Re-

---

[4]René Pache, *The Inspiration and Authority of Scripture* (Chicago: Moody Press, 1969), p. 45.

[5]Warren Vanhetloo, "Indications of Verbal Inspiration," *Calvary Baptist Theological Journal*, spring 1989, p. 63.

[6]B. B. Warfield, *The Inspiration and Authority of the Bible* (Philadelphia: The Presbyterian and Reformed Publishing Company, 1948), p. 133.

ceive ye the Holy Ghost" (John 20:22). Jesus thus associated divine breath with the Holy Spirit. In II Timothy 3:16, Paul relates God's breath to the Word of God. This word "God-breathed" appears to be tied to God's power.

Second, we understand this term in relation to communication. Warfield stressed that the term does not refer to "breathing in" but to "breathing out." In order to speak, we must draw breath, breathe it out across our vocal apparatus, and combine it with intelligent thought from the brain. God "breathed out" in communication with man, and the result is His Word.

Spirit-Inspired

Two major passages declare that the Holy Spirit is God's agent in inspiration. The prophets understood it was "the Spirit of Christ which was in them" who spoke through them (I Pet. 1:11). Peter further affirms that "holy men of God spake as they were moved by the Holy Ghost" (II Pet. 1:21). Other passages of Scripture teach the same truth. David claimed, "The Spirit of the Lord spake by me, and his word was in my tongue" (II Sam. 23:2). One of the titles for our Bible is "the sword of the Spirit" (Eph. 6:17).

Inspiration's Extent

Verbal Inspiration

Christians have historically believed in the inspiration of the Scripture, and they have historically emphasized that the very words of the Scripture were inspired. To see the historical roots of this doctrine, notice the words of John Gill, first published in 1769 and 1770.[7] Gill wrote before higher criticism appeared. He wrote before the current controversies over textual criticism and versions arose. He said, "Let it be

---

[7]John Gill, *Body of Divinity* (1769-70; reprint, Atlanta: Turner Lassetter, 1965), p. xix.

observed, that not the matter of the Scriptures only, but the very words in which they are written, are of God."[8] He goes on to explain,

> So it might be with the sacred writers, if words were not suggested to them, as well as matter; and then we should be left at an uncertainty about the real sense of the Holy Spirit, if not led into a wrong one; it seems, therefore, most agreeable, that words also, as well as matter, were given by divine inspiration. . . .[9]

Gill then cites Paul's words in I Corinthians 2:13: "Which things also we speak, not in the words which man's wisdom teacheth, but which the Holy Ghost teacheth."

The passage in II Timothy 3 also conveys the idea of verbal inspiration. In verse fifteen, Paul reminds Timothy "that from a child thou hast known the holy scriptures." The word translated "scriptures" is the Greek word "grammata," the word for "letters."[10] R.C.H. Lenski uses this verse to stress verbal inspiration, stating,

> Purposely Paul does not say ἅγιαι γράφαι, "Holy Scriptures," but γράμματα, "letters," "script." Little Timothy learned his ABC's from the Bible, learned to read from the Bible, and thus from earliest childhood spelled out "sacred letters.". . . *Gramma* is just a written character; the plural *[grammata]*, many of them as they make written words and thus convey sense [emphasis Lenski's].[11]

Even the words of the Scripture are holy. They are words the Holy Spirit spoke. We have seen that David claimed that the Spirit's words were in his mouth. We are told that the

---

[8]Ibid., p. 12.

[9]Ibid., pp. 12-13.

[10]William F. Arndt and F. Wilbur Gingrich, *A Greek-English Lexicon of the New Testament* (Chicago: The University of Chicago Press, 1957), p. 164.

[11]R.C.H. Lenski, *The Interpretation of St. Paul's Epistles to the Colossians, to the Thessalonians, to Timothy, to Titus, and to Philemon* (Minneapolis: Augsburg Publishing House, 1946), p. 839.

enigmatic Balaam spoke after "the Lord put a word in Balaam's mouth" (Num. 23:5). Monroe Parker asserts,

> Moses, himself, claimed inspiration for at least a part of the Pentateuch. In Deuteronomy he wrote, "And the Lord said unto Moses . . . Now, therefore, write ye this song for you, and teach it the children of Israel: put it in their mouths that this song may be a witness for me against the children of Israel" (Deut. 31:16, 19).[12]

Add to this the many times the prophets claimed the word of the Lord came to them or used the phrase "thus saith the Lord" and we must come to the conclusion that God's work of inspiration is verbal inspiration.

Plenary Inspiration

Paul clearly states, "All scripture is given by inspiration of God . . ." (II Tim. 3:16). All Scripture, and every part of it, is inspired. Charles Hodge succinctly describes this idea:

> Plenary is opposed to partial. The Church doctrine denies that inspiration is confined to parts of the Bible; and affirms that it applies to all the books of the sacred canon. It denies that the sacred writers were merely partially inspired; it asserts that they were fully inspired as to all that they teach, whether of doctrine or fact.[13]

Note Hodge's contention that all Scripture is inspired and that the authors of our Bible were inspired in all their *biblical* writings. Some of the biblical authors wrote more than God preserved for us in Scripture. Those extra-biblical writings are not inspired. The Spirit of God influenced the authors of Scripture as they wrote the words of the Bible. Thus the authors themselves were not inspired, but the words of Holy Scripture they penned are. The words of Scripture are "holy

[12]Monroe Parker, *More Desirable Than Gold* (Decatur, AL: self-published, 1963), p. 20.
[13]Charles Hodge, *Systematic Theology* (Grand Rapids: Wm. B. Eerdmans Publishing Company, 1993), I:165.

words" (II Tim. 3:15) and the sum total of the holy words, "all scripture is given by inspiration of God" (II Tim. 3:16). The Holy Spirit worked in and upon the authors of the Scripture to accurately and truthfully record the revelation God gave to men.

Inerrant Inspiration

Since God's Spirit gave us an inspired Word, it follows that the Scriptures must also be inerrant. We will use two words as synonyms. By the word "inerrant," theologians mean "without error."[14] Theologians also use the word "infallible" to indicate "unimpeachable authority."[15] These terms mean "that the authors wrote all God wanted them to write without error."[16] This doctrine has been the cause of a great battle within the ranks of New Evangelicalism in the last twenty-five years.[17] We cannot overestimate the importance of this doctrine. Erickson says, "In a real sense, it is the completion of the doctrine of Scripture."[18]

If we have an inspired Bible, then it logically follows that we must have an inerrant Bible. Our purpose is not to fully develop the doctrine here. It is enough to say that when the Bible claims to be "perfect," "right," "pure," and "clean" (Psa. 19:7-9), it must be inerrant. The Psalmist calls the Word God's "righteous judgments" (Psa. 119:62); Paul affirms that the law is "holy, and just, and good" (Rom. 7:12) and speaks of the "holy scriptures" (II Tim. 3:15). Peter says that God's

---

[14]Ernest Pickering, "Systematic Theology" (Minneapolis: Central Baptist Theological Seminary, 1963, lecture notes).

[15]Ibid.

[16]Ibid.

[17]That battle is outside the scope of this document. For details see Harold Lindsell, *The Battle for the Bible* (Grand Rapids: Zondervan Publishing House, 1976).

[18]Millard J. Erickson, *Christian Theology* (Grand Rapids: Baker Book House, 1985), p. 221.

revelation is the "holy commandment" (II Pet. 2:21). Logic demands the reasonable conclusion that God revealed His truth to men, inspired His Word, and gave it to us without error; as God's inerrant, infallible revelation, it is completely trustworthy.

This doctrine is not of new development. Erickson[19] shows that Christians have held to the inerrancy and infallibility of Scripture throughout church history.

An Original Inspiration

Scripture also teaches that the authors of Scripture experienced the ministry of the Holy Spirit, which produced an inspired Bible. Peter tells us, "but holy men of God spake as they were moved by the Holy Ghost" (II Pet. 1:21). The previously cited statements about Balaam and David confirm Peter's words, as do many other Scripture references. Christians have historically taught that inspiration extends to the original manuscripts, not to copies that scribes subsequently made for succeeding generations of believers. We could cite Warfield, Pache, Hodge, and others who have embraced this view. These men stand as a mere sampling in a long tradition of teaching on the subject.

The translators of the King James Version understood that only the original manuscripts were inspired. They made this revealing statement:

> No cause therefore why the word translated should be denied to be the word, or forbidden to be current, notwithstanding that some imperfections and blemishes may be noted in the setting forth of it. For what ever was perfect under the sun, where Apostles or apostolick men, that is, men endued with an extraordinary measure of God's

[19]Ibid., pp. 221-40.

> Spirit, and privileged with the privilege of infallibility, had not their hand?[20]

We should note that they understood that only "Apostles or apostolick men"[21] enjoyed the privilege of infallibility. They clearly did not attribute inspiration to subsequent copies of the original manuscripts.

The translators also spoke of the imperfections of any translation, illustrating it by a hypothetical speech their king might make before Parliament. Though made in English, the speech translated into "*French, Dutch, Italian and Latin* is still the King's speech, though it be not interpreted by every translator with the like grace" [emphasis theirs].[22] They clearly understood only the original manuscripts to be inspired, and yet they could trust the reliability of translations.

We are dealing with important material. Yet the translators of the King James Version, speaking of their own work, illustrated their point with a homey illustration that causes us to smile:

> A man may be counted a virtuous man, though he have made many slips in his life, (else there were none virtuous, for *in many things we offend all*), also a comely man and lovely, though he have some warts upon his hand; yea, not only freckles upon his face, but also scars. No cause therefore why the word translated should be denied to be the word, or forbidden to be current, notwithstanding that some imperfections and blemishes may be noted in the setting forth of it.[23]

These men clearly understood that despite imperfections, a translation is still reliable and to be regarded as authentically

---

[20]"The Translators to the Reader" in *The Holy Bible, a facsimile in a reduced size of the Authorized Version published in the year 1611* (Oxford: Oxford University Press, 1911), p. 106.

[21]Ibid.

[22]Ibid.

[23]Ibid.

the Word of God. They also affirmed their belief that only the words originally penned by the authors of the Scripture were so breathed out by the Holy Spirit as to be infallible. They attributed infallibility not to translations, not even to the authors, but to the God-breathed original manuscripts.

Gill spoke clearly concerning inspiration:

> This is to be understood of the Scriptures, as in the original languages in which they were written, and not of translations; unless it could be thought, that the translators of the Bible into the several languages of the nations into which it has been translated, were under the divine inspiration also in translating, and were directed of God to the use of words they have rendered the original by; *but this is not reasonable to suppose* [emphasis mine].[24]

Gill writes extensively on this subject. He affirms that every translation must be brought to the original languages of the Scripture and by them "be examined, tried, and judged, and to be corrected and amended: and if this was not the case, we should have no certain and infallible rule to go by."[25] He goes on to discount the Catholic position established at the Council of Trent, that the Latin Vulgate is "authentic," and denies the assertion of Trent that the originals should be corrected by the Latin translation![26] Gill then assures his readers that popular translations are reliable:

> For whenever a set of men have been engaged in this work, as were in our nation, men well skilled in the languages, and partakers of the grace of God; of sound principles, and of integrity and faithfulness, having the fear of God before their eyes; they have never failed of producing a translation worthy of acceptation; and in which, though they have mistook some words and phrases, and erred in some lesser and lighter matters; yet not so as to affect any

---

[24]Gill, p. 13.
[25]Ibid.
[26]Ibid.

momentous article of faith or practice; and therefore such translations as ours may be regarded as the rule of faith.[27]

Gill's work was first published in 1769-70, 158 years after the King James Version was translated.[28] His writing followed the adoption of the London Confession by 102 years. If anyone viewed the translation as inspired and on a par with the original manuscripts, it seems that such a doctrine would have been developed and advocated by that time.

Space limits this discussion, but the facts are clear. Scripture teaches that the Holy Spirit moved the authors of the Scripture. Christians have affirmed that truth for centuries. Translations or translators cannot claim the privilege of the same ministry of God's Spirit. Yet when God-fearing men put their hand to the task, they are able to produce a reliable translation that believers can, in every sense, trust as the infallible Word of God.

Preservation

The second of "those things which are most surely believed among us" (Luke 1:1) concerning God's Word is the fact of preservation. Fundamentalists and conservative evangelicals accept the idea that God has providentially preserved His Word from the time of its writing to our present time. The Westminster Confession and Catechisms, adopted in 1646, "became the dominant standards of Presbyterianism in the English-speaking world."[29] The confession speaks eloquently:

> The Old Testament in Hebrew (which was the native language of the people of God of old), and the New Testa-

---

[27]Ibid.

[28]Gill, xix.

[29]John H. Leith, ed., *Creeds of the Churches* (Garden City, NY: Doubleday and Company, Inc., 1963), p. 192.

ment in Greek (which at the time of the writing of it was most generally known to the nations), being immediately inspired by God, and by his singular care and providence kept pure in all ages, and therefore authentical; so as in all controversies of religion the Church is finally to appeal unto them.[30]

The Baptists of London adopted their Second London Confession in 1677. In writing this statement, they borrowed heavily from the Westminster Confession. Their confession opens with a line the Westminster Confession did not contain. Affirming the Baptists' belief in the sole authority of Scripture, it says, "The Holy Scripture is the only sufficient, certain, and infallible rule of all saving Knowledge, Faith, and Obedience. . . ."[31] The statement on the inspiration and preservation of Scripture is borrowed from the Westminster Confession without any change. The Baptists cited Isaiah 8:20 as a reference for the authenticity of Scripture. They also used Acts 15:15 to support the statement that Scripture is the final appeal for all religious controversies.[32] Thus our own generation of Christians is not the first to wrestle with the issue of preservation.

Providential Preservation

Believers have distinguished between inspiration and preservation in one important area. Scripture teaches that inspiration is a supernatural work of God through His Holy Spirit. Preservation is not a supernatural, but rather a providential, work of God. The Westminster Confession and the Second London Confession both used the word "providence"

---

[30]Leith, p. 196.
[31]L. Russ Bush and Tom J. Nettles, *Baptists and the Bible* (Chicago: Moody Press, 1980), p. 65.
[32]William L. Lumpkin, *Baptist Confessions of Faith* (Philadelphia: The Judson Press, 1959), p. 251.

in describing God's protection and preservation of His Word. Millard Erickson describes providence:

> While creation is God's originating work with respect to the universe, providence is his continuing relationship to it. By providence we mean the continuing action of God by which he preserves in existence the creation which he has brought into being, and guides it to his intended purposes for it.[33]

Erickson goes on to distinguish two aspects of God's preservation. One aspect is that God sustains His creation, and the other is His "activity in guiding and directing the course of events to fulfill the purposes which he has in mind."[34] Rolland McCune clearly describes the difference between the miraculous and the providential, saying, "A miracle is a *direct* application of God's power into our time-space-mass continuum. A work of God's providence is indirect, through secondary causation" [emphasis McCune's].[35]

With this understanding, we turn to another old writer to aid our understanding of the providential preservation of Scripture. John Leadley Dagg (1794-1884) wrote an early American systematic theology. His *Manual of Theology and Church Order* survives in print. Paige Patterson says his works "represented the first full system of theology prepared by a Baptist in America."[36] Writing in 1857, Dagg distinguished between God's miraculous and providential activity:

> A miracle was needed in the original production of the Scriptures; and, accordingly, a miracle was wrought; but the preservation of the inspired word, in as much perfection as was necessary to answer the purpose for which it

---

[33]Erickson, p. 387.
[34]Ibid., p. 388.
[35]Rolland D. McCune, "Systematic Theology I" (Detroit Baptist Theological Seminary, class syllabus), p. 28.
[36]Paige Patterson in John L. Dagg, *Manual of Theology and Church Order* (Harrisonburg, VA, 1982), flyleaf.

was given, did not require a miracle, and accordingly it was committed to the providence of God. Yet the providence which has preserved the divine oracles, has been special and remarkable.[37]

Sixty-two years later Kyle, in his Philadelphia address, would say,

But we have not yet reached the bounds of this text. From everlasting God's Word is true, and to everlasting it endures.

Here is a word that has perpetuity, ay, it has eternity. Solomon has said that God has "set eternity in the heart." Surely this is true of the heart in which His Word is hidden. What a priceless treasure in a world of fleeting change![38]

The Fact of Preservation

Every orthodox writer I have read on the subject of the Scriptures affirms his belief in the providential preservation of the Bible. There is, however, a division among men over whether this providential preservation is taught in the Bible.

Daniel B. Wallace takes the position that Scripture does not teach its own preservation. He cites five passages (Psa. 119:89; Isa. 40:8; Matt. 5:17-18; John 10:35; and I Pet. 1:23-25) commonly used to support the preservation of Scripture. He contends that these passages used to support the Bible's preservation are misapplied or taken out of context. Wallace says,

My own preference is to speak of God's providential care of the text as can be seen throughout church history, without elevating such to the level of doctrine. If this makes us theologically uncomfortable, it should at the same time make us at ease historically, for the NT is the most remarkably preserved text of the ancient world—

---

[37]Dagg, p. 24.
[38]Kyle, p. 79.

both in terms of the quantity of manuscripts and in their temporal proximity to the originals.[39]

Please notice that *Wallace does not deny that God has pre-served His Word*. However, he does not believe that Scripture teaches that preservation. History does demonstrate God's providential preservation of His Word. We agree with Wallace that history demonstrates preservation and do not argue that point. The survival of over five thousand manuscripts containing part or all of the New Testament alone affirms it. The fact of preservation leads us to the conclusion that in the overwhelming majority of cases, we are certain of the precise wording of the original manuscripts. It should assure us that we possess the very words God gave.

We fervently disagree with Wallace when he says that Scripture does not teach its own preservation. That leads us to consider the biblical evidence on this subject.

Biblical Proofs for Preservation

1 Peter 1:23-25
> Being born again, not of corruptible seed, but of incorruptible, by the word of God, which liveth and abideth for ever. For all flesh is as grass, and all the glory of man as the flower of grass. The grass withereth, and the flower thereof falleth away: But the word of the Lord endureth for ever. And this is the word which by the gospel is preached unto you.

Peter quotes Isaiah when he affirms that God's Word is indestructible. Isaiah says, "The grass withereth, the flower

---

[39]Daniel B. Wallace, "Inspiration, Preservation, and New Testament Textual Criticism" in. Gary T. Meadors, ed., *New Testament Essays* (Winona Lake, IN: BMH Books, 1991), p. 84. This article was also printed as "Inspiration, Preservation, and New Testament Textual Criticism," in *Grace Theological Journal* 12 (1992), pp. 21-51.

fadeth: but the word of our God shall stand for ever" (Isa. 40:8). This statement, in my understanding, is unequivocal. Wallace objects to the use of verse twenty-five, saying it "uses ῥῆμα [rhema] (not λόγος [logos])—a term which typically refers to the spoken word."[40] We must object to Wallace's argument here for two reasons. First, it is true that *logos* normally refers to the written word and *rhema* is the Greek word that commonly indicates the spoken word. However, *rhema* is clearly used in a broader sense also. The word *rhema* appears about seventy times in the New Testament.[41] Vine says the word is "used of the gospel."[42] Arndt and Gingrich say that *rhema* refers to "the word of God" in Romans 10:17.[43] Paul uses this word several times in Romans 10. He calls the message of Christ "the word of faith, which we preach" (v. 8). Paul says, "So then, faith cometh by hearing, and hearing by the word of God" (v. 17). Both verses use the word Peter uses in I Peter 1:23-25. Surely they refer to the message of the gospel, and verse seventeen is universally taken to be a reference to God's Word. The Romans 10 passage and Peter's statement each emphasize the Word as it was preached. Perhaps this is why the Holy Spirit chose the Greek word *rhema* for use in each passage.[44] Reasonable interpretation can accept Peter's statements as a reference to the whole of Scripture and as a promise that God has preserved His word for men.

Also, Paul uses *rhema* in what must be references to the body of Scripture in Ephesians 5:26 ("the washing of water by

---

[40]Wallace, p. 84.

[41]George V. Wigram, *The Englishman's Greek Concordance of the New Testament*, 9th ed. (London: Samuel Bagster and Sons, 1903), p. 677.

[42]W. E. Vine, *Expository Dictionary of New Testament Words* (Westwood, NJ: Fleming H. Revell Company, 1966), IV:230.

[43]William F. Arndt and F. Wilbur Gingrich, *A Greek-English Lexicon of the New Testament* (Chicago: The University of Chicago Press, 1957), p. 742.

[44]W. E. Vine, IV:230, states that *rhema* refers "to the individual Scripture which the Spirit brings to our remembrance for use in time of need, a prerequisite being the regular storing of the mind with Scripture."

the word") and in Ephesians 6:17 ("the sword of the Spirit, which is the word of God"). These statements must reasonably be taken as references to the entire body of Scripture. The statement in Hebrews 6:5 ("and have tasted the good word of God") is also another passage where *rhema* is probably used of the entire volume of Scripture. So while *logos* normally refers to the written word, and *rhema* normally refers to the spoken word, such usages are not hard and fast. The inspired Word uses *rhema* to speak of the written Word of God in several clear passages. Scripture employs *logos* and *rhema* as synonyms several times.

Grant Osborne provides an informative insight at this point. He comments on the danger of making too much of the difference between synonyms. He states,

> A basic error of many exegetes is to emphasize the differences of meaning between synonymous terms found in a list; for instance, the terms for "love" in John 21:15-17, the types of sacrifice in Hebrews 10:8; or the terms for prayer in Philippians 4:6. We must at all times be aware of the possibility that the reason for the employment of different terms or phrases may be stylistic rather than theological; repetition may have been used for emphasis, and the differences between the words should not be stressed.[45]

Second, Peter uses both *logos* and *rhema* to refer to God's Word in this passage. In verse twenty-three he says the new birth comes "by the word (*logos*) of God, which liveth and abideth forever." He affirms this truth after quoting Isaiah 40:8, which is a clear reference to the written, prophetic Word of God as given in the Old Testament. Then in verse twenty-five, he says that "the word (*rhema*) of the Lord endureth forever. And this is the word (*rhema*) which by the

---

[45]Grant R. Osborne, *The Hermeneutical Spiral* (Downers Grove, IL: InterVarsity Press, 1991), p. 36.

gospel is preached unto you." Peter uses *logos* to speak of the written Word of God that works the new birth in verse twenty-three, and he then uses *rhema* to say that the Word of God, having been preached as gospel to men, will remain into the ages. We conclude that in this passage the Holy Spirit uses the two words as synonyms to speak of the written Word of God. This is similar to Paul's statement in II Thessalonians 2:15 where he speaks of the *paradosis* or revelation he gave the Thessalonians "whether by word, or our epistle." Whether delivered by the spoken word of the apostle or by his written epistle, the revelation from God was authoritative. This passage also leads us to conclude that God has preserved the very Word that is the agent of the new birth and the message of the gospel.

Twice in I Peter 1:23-25 Peter declares that God's Word "abideth forever" and "endureth forever" (vv. 23, 25). He uses the same word in each verse. It means "to remain in a place, to tarry," and the opposite is "to go away."[46] The Holy Spirit uses the word to describe "the eternal God" and "the unchanging and perfect Word of God."[47] God's Word will not go away; rather, it remains. And God tells us through Peter that it remains "forever" (vv. 23, 25). His emphasis here is upon the fact that God's Word is eternal and preserved forever. Perhaps Peter remembered the words of Christ when He said,

> Think not that I am come to destroy the law, or the prophets: I am not come to destroy, but to fulfil. For verily I say unto you, Till heaven and earth pass, one jot or one tittle shall in no wise pass from the law, till all be fulfilled (Matt. 5:17, 18).

This verse certainly makes its primary focus the fulfillment of Scripture. Yet, McCune rightly states, "Also, the idea

---

[46]R. Bultmann, "μένω" in Gerhard Kittel, ed., *Theological Dictionary of the New Testament* (reprint, Grand Rapids: Wm. B. Eerdmans Publishing Co., 1975), IV:574.
[47]Ibid.

of preservation is strongly implied in the texts that speak of the continuing authority of the Word of God (Matt. 5:18; John 10:35; I Pet. 1:9-13)."[48]

Because God has preserved Scripture eternally, Peter can assure his readers that it is "a more sure word of prophecy" than even his eyewitness account of Christ's transfiguration (II Pet. 1:16-19). Scripture's truthfulness and reliability rest upon the fact that God revealed its truth, inspired its writing, and preserved its words forever.

Wallace is a respected Greek scholar. I have cited one of his books in this study and used it many times with profit. He has been very kind in private correspondence about this issue. At this point, however, he appears to have used a general distinction that does not apply to this passage.[49] We can claim I Peter 1:23-25 as an unequivocal biblical affirmation that God has preserved His Word.

Further Scriptural Evidence

As noted, Wallace names five passages that "are adduced as proof that preservation refers to the written Word of God: Ps 119:89, Isa 40:8, Matt 5:17-18, John 10:35, and 1 Pet 1:23-25."[50]

Rolland McCune elaborates on the issue of preservation, and he names three more of these passages in his comments:

Also the idea of preservation is strongly implied in the texts that speak of the continuing authority of the Word

---

[48]McCune, pp. 28-29.

[49]Patrick J. Hurley, *A Concise Introduction to Logic* (Belmont, CA: Wadsworth Publishing Company, 1988), p. 113, says, "The fallacy of accident is committed when a general rule is applied wrongly to a specific case. Typically, the general rule is cited (either directly or implicitly) in the premises and then wrongly applied to the specific case mentioned in the conclusion. Because of the 'accidental' features of the specific case, the general rule does not fit." Wallace's statement appears to be a textbook example of this fallacy.

[50]Wallace, p. 84.

of God (Matt 5:18; John 10:35; 1 Pet. 1:9-13). What the prophets wrote is part of the divine record and continuously stands as the authoritative, indestructible Word of God. Preservation is implied in the warnings against corrupting the text or against neutralizing the message of the text, and implied in the commands to study and know the Scripture . . . While the Bible teaches the ultimate indestructibility of God's verbal revelation (Matt 24:35; John 10:35; 1 Pet 1:25), and this in itself would seem to imply some kind of a process of preservation, the Bible does not state how or where the manuscript lineage of that written revelation is being preserved.[51]

The Matthew and John passages certainly imply, if they do not directly teach, the preservation of God's Word.

The Record of Biblical History
Beyond the clear statement of I Peter and the supporting evidence of the other passages, Scripture gives some historical record that God has providentially preserved His Word. We need to understand that Scripture records varied methods God has used in preserving His Word. Hilkiah the high priest and Shaphan the scribe came to young King Josiah with what was apparently the only surviving copy of the book of the Law (II Kings 22:8, 9). God providentially protected and preserved *just one copy* at that time. Years later the godless King Jehoiakim used his penknife and fireplace to destroy the divine revelation. God instructed Jeremiah, "Take thee again another roll, and write in it all the former words that were in the first roll, which Jehoiakim the king of Judah hath burned" (Jer. 36:28). In this case we *know* we do not have the original manuscript, but we are sure we do have the very Word of God preserved for us. Conversely, for the New Testament 5,500 manuscripts give eloquent testimony that God has preserved His Word. Whether God preserved but one copy, replicated

---

[51]McCune, pp. 28-29.

what a reprobate king destroyed, or preserved thousands of manuscripts for our study, the lesson is the same. The providence of an all-knowing, omnipotent God was and is sufficient to preserve His Word. And He has preserved it!

Issues Related to Preservation

The Method of Preservation

The great debate today among Fundamentalists and conservative evangelicals is not really *whether* God has preserved His Word but *how* He did it. God provides detailed information about how He inspired His Word, but Scripture is silent about the method of preservation. McCune's statement that "the Bible does not state how or where the manuscript lineage of that written revelation is being preserved"[52] is incontrovertible. That issue should not be the source of the bitter contention and division it is becoming in many circles. If the Bible is silent on the issue of how God preserved His Word, then it seems ludicrous that some make it a test of fellowship or more.

Textual Variants

The existing manuscripts reveal that variations exist among them. These variants exist because humans copied the manuscripts; therefore, variations were inevitable. William W. Combs states, "This is easily demonstrated from the evidence. For instance, we presently possess over 5000 copies, or partial copies, of the Greek NT, and no two of these manuscripts agree exactly."[53] However, comparison of the manuscripts also reveals amazing agreement. The conclusion of most scholars is that God preserved His Word in the manuscripts we have. We can rest assured that despite the textual variants, we have

---

[52]McCune, p. 29.

[53]William W. Combs, "Errors in the King James Version?" *Detroit Baptist Seminary Journal*, fall 1999, p. 160.

the very words the authors of Scripture penned as the Holy Spirit moved them. In the vast majority of cases, we know exactly what that wording is. This issue of current debate (and often bitter contention) was comprehended by men of former generations. For years biblical scholars have stated that in only a few instances do these variants create any question concerning the reading of a text. Where the readings are uncertain, no article of faith or tenet of biblical Christianity is harmed.

Further, it is important to note that the old writers were aware of the textual variations that produce so much debate and contention today. They were not overly concerned with those variations. Dagg assures us that we can trust our translations. He says,

> The consequence is, that, although the various readings found in the existing manuscripts, are numerous, we are able in every case, to determine the correct reading, so far as is necessary for the establishment of our faith, or the direction of our practice in every important particular. So little, after all, do the copies differ from each other, that these minute differences, when viewed in contrast with their general agreement, render the fact of that agreement the more impressive, and may be said to serve practically, rather to increase, than impair our confidence in their general correctness. . . . As copies of the Holy Scriptures, though made by fallible hands, are sufficient for our guidance in the study of divine truth; so translations, though made with uninspired human skill, are sufficient for those who have not access to the inspired original.[54]

James M. Gray served as president of Moody Bible Institute many years ago. Writing on the subject of inspiration in *The Fundamentals*, Gray spoke to this issue. He said,

---

[54]Dagg, pp. 24-25.

But if this question be so purely speculative and valueless, what becomes of the science of biblical criticism by which properly we set such store today? Do builders drive piles into soft earth if they never expect to touch bottom? Do scholars dispute about the Scripture text and minutely examine the history and meaning of single words, "the delicate coloring of mood, tense and accent," if at the end there is no approximation to an absolute?

Nor is that original parchment so remote a thing as some suppose. Do not the number and variety of manuscripts and versions extant render it comparatively easy to arrive at a knowledge of its text, and does not competent scholarship today affirm that as to the New Testament at least, we have in 999 cases out of every thousand the very word of the original text? Let candid consideration be given to these things, and it will be seen that we are not pursuing a phantom in contending for an inspired autograph of the Bible.[55]

Gray later argues in the same vein, pointing out that Paul turns an entire argument on a single letter in Galatians 3:16.[56] The blessings of justification are received through Abraham's *seed*, not his *seeds*. Such reasoning and argumentation from the authors of Scripture is futile unless God both inspired and preserved for us the wording of Scripture.

Combs, a respected New Testament scholar, states the same thing as Gray:

Clearly, the original scrolls and codices have long since perished, but that does not mean we do not have access to the original words themselves. It does not mean we are in doubt about every word in the Hebrew/Aramaic and Greek texts we do have. And while there is disagreement

---

[55]James M. Gray, "The Inspiration of the Bible—Definition, Extent and Proof" in R. A. Torrey, ed., *The Fundamentals* (Grand Rapids: Kregel Classics, 1958), p. 140.

[56]The difference is one letter in our English translation, and in the Greek text is the difference between σπέρμασιν and σπέρματι.

over which printed Hebrew/Aramaic and Greek texts are closest to the autographs, most reasonable people would be willing to concede that where all extant manuscripts are in agreement, we can safely conclude that we *do* have the text of the autographs.[57]

A current theologian echoes the same position. Wayne Grudem states:

> This is not to say that the study of textual variants is unimportant, but it is to say that the study of textual variants has not left us in confusion about what the original manuscripts said. It has rather brought us extremely close to the content of those original manuscripts. For most practical purposes, then, the *current published scholarly texts* of the Hebrew Old Testament and Greek New Testament *are the same as the original manuscripts.* Thus, when we say that the original manuscripts were inerrant, we are also implying that over 99 percent of the words in our present manuscripts are also inerrant, for they are exact copies of the originals. Furthermore, we *know* where the uncertain readings are (for where there are no textual variants we have no reason to expect faulty copying of the original). Thus, our present manuscripts are for most purposes the same as the original manuscripts, and the doctrine of inerrancy therefore directly concerns our present manuscripts as well [emphasis Grudem's].[58]

We can rest assured today that God revealed His truth to men, inspired its writing in an inerrant, infallible book, and preserved it for our use to His glory.

The Textual Debate

Our purpose is not to enter the debate over manuscripts and modern translations in this book. Those discussions are large and beyond the scope of this discussion. We should note

---

[57]Combs, p. 154.

[58]Wayne Grudem, *Systematic Theology: An Introduction to Biblical Doctrine* (Grand Rapids: Zondervan Publishing House, 1994), p. 96.

that since God has preserved His Word, and since the manuscripts give such an accurate record of that Word, the debate whether to use the Textus Receptus, the Majority Text, or the Critical Text[59] should not be a source of bitter contention. Neither should it be a test of fellowship among brethren. This is not to demean the textual variants. The issue is worthy of continued study, and scholars should pursue the accurate wording of the original writings in those areas where uncertainty exists. Perhaps more evidence will be discovered to enlighten believers regarding some texts in those areas where variants exist. It could also be that part of the debate with some of the variant readings owes to the limitations of our finite minds. The issue should not be as divisive as many have let it become.[60]

Illumination

Illumination can be simply defined as "that influence or ministry of the Holy Spirit which enables all who are in right relation with God to understand the objective written revelation."[61] The translators of the King James Version described the Holy Spirit's teaching work:

It remaineth that we commend thee to God, and to the Spirit of his grace, which is able to build further than we

---

[59]For reading on this issue, the Textus Receptus viewpoint is represented best by Edward F. Hills, *The King James Version Defended* (Des Moines: The Christian Research Press, 1984). Wilbur Pickering, *The Identity of the New Testament Text* (Nashville: Thomas Nelson Publishers, 1977), advocates the Majority Text position. James R. White presents the Critical Text position in *The King James Only Controversy* (Minneapolis: Bethany House Publishers, 1995).

[60]For a fair, reasoned, and comprehensive treatment of the issues relating to this controversy see James B. Williams, ed., *From the Mind of God to the Mind of Man: A Layman's Guide to How We Got Our Bible* (Greenville, SC: Ambassador-Emerald International, 1999).

[61]Merrill F. Unger, *Introductory Guide to the Old Testament* (Grand Rapids: Zondervan Publishing House, 1956), p. 24.

can ask or think. He removeth the scales from our eyes, the vail from our hearts, opening our wits that we may understand his word, enlarging our hearts, yea, correcting our affections, that we may love it above gold and silver, yea, that we may love it to the end.[62]

Dagg described something of this work as well:

A full conviction that the Bible is the word of God, is necessary to give us confidence in its teachings, and respect for its decisions. With this conviction pervading the mind when we read the sacred pages, we realize that God is speaking to us, and when we feel the truth take hold of our hearts, we know that it is God with whom we have to do.[63]

Illumination and the Sinner

Jesus promised His disciples that the Spirit of God would indwell them. Part of the Spirit's work *in* the believer is to work *through* the believer in the world. Jesus said: "And when he is come, he will reprove the world of sin, and of righteousness, and of judgment" (John 16:8). We understand that reproving work to be the work of convicting lost men. The Holy Spirit convinces men of their sin, of Christ's finished work, and of inescapable judgment. The Holy Spirit must bring this conviction before a sinner will turn to Christ.[64]

Illumination and the Saint

Jesus continued His description of the Spirit's illuminating work when He said,

---

[62]"The Translators to the Readers," pp. 109-10.

[63]Dagg, p. 25.

[64]Most theologians and commentators do not include the Spirit's work in convicting sinners as part of His illuminating work. However, this is an emphasis Dr. Ernest Pickering made in my Systematic Theology classes years ago. In a September 30, 1999, telephone interview about this subject, he stated that Dr. Lewis Sperry Chafer also approached the subject in this way. Merrill C. Tenney, "The

> Howbeit when he, the Spirit of truth, is come, he will guide you into all truth: for he shall not speak of himself; but whatsoever he shall hear, that shall he speak: and he will shew you things to come. He shall glorify me: for he shall receive of mine, and shall shew it unto you. All things that the Father hath are mine: therefore said I, that he shall take of mine, and shall shew it unto you. (John 16:13-15).[65]

Paul gave us the classic passage on this subject.

> But as it is written, Eye hath not seen, nor ear heard, neither have entered into the heart of man, the things which God hath prepared for them that love him. But God hath revealed them unto us by his Spirit: for the Spirit searcheth all things, yea the deep things of God. For what man knoweth the things of a man, save the spirit of man which is in him? Even so the things of God knoweth no man, but the Spirit of God. Now we have received, not the spirit of the world, but the spirit which is of God; that we might know the things that are freely given to us of God. Which things also we speak, not in the words which man's wisdom teacheth, but which the Holy Ghost teacheth; comparing spiritual things with spiritual (I Cor. 2:9-13).

The Spirit of God indwells believers, and one of His ministries to us is "that we might know the things that are freely

---

Gospel of John" in Frank E. Gaebelein, ed., *The Expositor's Bible Commentary* (Grand Rapids: Zondervan Publishing House, 1981), 9:157-58, also sees the entire John 16:8-15 passage as a unit dealing with "three major aspects of the ministry of the Holy Spirit." They are: "1. To the world—conviction of sin, righteousness and judgment. 2. To the disciples—direction and truth. 3. To Jesus—revealing him more perfectly to and through those who represent him." Treating this passage in this way is not without precedent.

[65]Some Bible students do not use this passage to justify the Spirit's illuminating work. They cite the phrase "he will shew you things to come" (v. 13) as a clear reference to the Spirit's work of revelation to the apostles. That point is granted.

Yet Charles C. Ryrie in *Basic Theology* (Wheaton, IL: Victor Books, 1986), p. 116, cites it, saying that "two principal passages describe this ministry of the Spirit (John 16:12-15 and 1 Cor. 2:9–3:2)."

given to us of God" (I Cor. 2:12). The next verse elaborates, "Which things also we speak, not in the words which man's wisdom teacheth, but which the Holy Ghost teacheth; comparing spiritual things with spiritual" (I Cor. 2:13). God the Holy Spirit is the believer's teacher (I John 2:27). As we study God's Word, the Holy Spirit teaches us the revealed, inspired truth. This teaching ministry encompasses "all truth" (John 16:13).[66] In the Word, we see God in His glory, and we see ourselves (II Cor. 3:18; James 1:22-25). God desires that as we learn the truth of His Word by His Spirit, we obey it (James 1:22, 25). God has a definite goal in mind as the Holy Spirit performs this work in believers. His goal is that we be changed into the likeness of His glory. "But we all, with open face beholding as in a glass the glory of the Lord, are changed into the same image from glory to glory, even as by the Spirit of the Lord" (II Cor. 3:18).

> Anoint mine eyes,
> O Holy Dove!
> That I may prize
> This Book of love.
>
> Unstop mine ears
> Made deaf by sin,
> That I may hear
> Thy voice within.
>
> Break my hard heart,
> Jesus, my Lord;
> In the inmost part
> Hide thy sweet Word.
>
> –Robert Murray M'Cheyne

---

[66]Ibid.

Conclusion

We see that God has not only communicated with men, but that He has also supernaturally inspired the writing of His truth. He has providentially preserved that truth for us, and by His Spirit, who indwells every born-again person, graciously teaches that truth to His children.

We can only stand in absolute awe at the magnitude of God's self-disclosure to sinful men. Our faith stands on God's revelation that first showed Himself to us, convicted us of our sin, powerfully drew us to the Savior, and effectively gives "us all things that pertain unto life and godliness" (II Pet. 1:3).

> "The grass withereth, the flower fadeth; . . . surely the people is grass; but the Word of our God shall stand forever." And when the "heavens shall roll together as a scroll, and the elements shall melt with fervent heat," that most stupendous of physical changes, and most fraught with momentous consequence, will itself be but the fulfillment of this great, almighty Word which liveth and abideth forever.[67]

---

[67]Kyle, p. 80.

THE FUNDAMENTALISTS' FIGHT

Hammer away ye rebel bands
Your hammers break, God's Anvil stands.

Last eve I paused beside the blacksmith's door,
And heard the anvil ring the vesper chime;
Then looking in, I saw upon the floor
Old hammers worn with beating years of time.

"How many anvils have you had," said I,
"To wear and batter all these hammers so?"
"Just one," said he, and then with twinkling eye,
"The anvil wears the hammer out, you know."

"And so," I thought, "The Anvil of God's Word
For ages skeptic blows have beat upon,
Yet, though the noise of falling blows was heard,
The Anvil is unharmed, the hammers gone."[1]

Beloved, when I gave all diligence to write unto you of the common salvation, it was needful for me to write unto you, *and exhort you that ye should earnestly contend for the faith* which was once delivered unto the saints (Jude 3) [emphasis mine].

New Testament Christianity stands on the foundation of a revealed message from God. In the same sentence in which Jude describes the foundation of a revealed Word, he exhorts Christians to earnestly contend for that faith. He introduces an element into Christianity that analysts have uniformly identified in modern Fundamentalism: a militant spirit.

---

[1]John Clifford in John R. Rice, ed., *Poems That Speak* (Murfreesboro, TN: Sword of the Lord Publishers, 1952), n.p. Used by permission.

Militance is a necessary, greatly misunderstood, and oft opposed part of our faith and heritage.

Chester E. Tulga described the reason Fundamentalism was naturally militant. Speaking at the twenty-fifth anniversary conference of the General Association of Regular Baptist Churches, he gave four reasons why militancy characterizes Fundamentalism:

1. Fundamentalism was a protest movement and naturally was militant in spirit and method.
2. This militancy was increased and deepened by the conviction of Fundamentalists that the spirit of their times was influenced by Satan, and like Luther, they were very conscious of his influence and activity.
3. The Fundamentalists refused to accommodate Christianity to the notions of their times.
4. The older Fundamentalists had a strong sense of the exceeding sinfulness of sin.[2]

Tulga's words are timeless. Each reason he cites for the militancy of those early Fundamentalists commends itself to their present-day heirs as a reason for militance in the present struggle.

The Case for Militance

Jude eloquently presents his case for militance by the use of the words "earnestly contend." The English language requires two words to convey the meaning of the one Greek word *epagonizomai*. This word comes from the word *agonizomai*, which entered the English language as "agony" and "agonize." It is an intense word, and its New Testament use is somewhat different from its English connotation. The word

---

[2]Chester E. Tulga, "The Fundamentalism of Yesterday, the Evangelicalism of Today, and the Fundamentalism of Tomorrow," *Testimonies*, May 1998, p. 7.

means "to carry on a conflict, contest, debate or legal suit."[3] It appears in the New Testament with several prefixes but always "has the same shades of meaning as the noun, and is sometimes used literally, sometimes figuratively."[4] *Agonizomai* provides the basis for a fascinating study of the Christian life. Our purpose here is to see how the inspired New Testament writers used it in relationship to "the faith."

The Christian Life a Contest

The noun *agon* is used in a familiar portion of Scripture. The author of Hebrews exhorts believers to "run with patience the race that is set before us" (Heb. 12:1). The Christian life is a contest, and believers must approach it with that attitude. Believers are in a struggle because of their faith in Christ (Heb. 10:32-34). Scripture uses Jude's word for "contend" three times to describe the struggle. The author of Hebrews describes the heroes of the faith by saying,

> And what shall I more say? for the time would fail me to tell of Gedeon, and of Barak, and of Samson, and of Jephthae; and of David also, and Samuel, and of the prophets: Who through faith subdued kingdoms, wrought righteousness, obtained promises, stopped the mouths of lions, Quenched the violence of fire, escaped the edge of the sword, out of weakness were made strong, waxed valiant in fight, turned to flight the armies of the aliens (Heb. 11:32-34).

A common denominator presents itself in the list of men whom the author of Hebrews names in these verses. They each fought or preached against the practices of idolatrous, God-hating, God-denying nations. They stood for God against these heathen nations. The battle was not merely a

---

[3]Ethelbert Stauffer, "ἀγών, ἀγωνίζομαι and Compounds," in Gerhard Kittel, ed., *Theological Dictionary of the New Testament* (Grand Rapids: Wm. B. Eerdmans Publishing Company, 1964), I:135.
[4]Ibid.

CONTENDING FOR THE FAITH

battle between nations or political forces. It raged between God and those who denied Him. These heroes of faith, believing God and His promises, "subdued kingdoms" (Heb. 11:33). The word *subdued* is Jude's word *contend*. These men contended for the true God against the "armies of the aliens" (Heb. 11:34). God calls on Christians to walk by faith even when persecuted (Heb. 11:36-40).

The writer of sacred Scripture then proceeds to the next logical truth. Present-day believers, cheered by the example of the heroes of another day, are to "run with patience the race that is set before us" (Heb. 12:1). The word *race* is the noun form of Jude's verb *contend*. The Christian life is a contested race, and every ounce of energy must be expended to reach the goal (Heb. 12:1). Believers must approach the entire Christian life with a militant attitude. We must stand, as did the heroes of faith before us, against the forces of ungodliness that attack our cause and our individual lives.

One more truth confronts us as we see the Christian life as a contest. The struggle in this race is against sin. The biblical author cites the example of our Savior, the Lord Jesus. He suffered at the hands of sinners when He died for them (Heb. 12:2, 3). Then the writer turns to Christians, saying, "Ye have not yet resisted unto blood, striving against sin" (Heb. 12:4). Jesus did resist unto blood, but we are in the same battle. We are *striving* against sin. That word is the same word that is translated *contend* in Jude 3. Christians must view their sojourn on earth as a contest, a battle against the forces of ungodliness and evil, yes, against sin itself. Believers will certainly end up as defeated, cold, indifferent, backslidden Christians unless they approach the Christian life with a militant spirit. So militance is not just an approach to the revealed Word and those who deny it. Scripture requires a militant spirit in reference to the entire Christian walk.

Suffering for the Faith

Philippians 1:27-30

The theme of Philippians 1 is evangelism. Paul wanted to hear that the Philippian believers were "striving together for the faith of the gospel" (Phil. 1:27). The word *agonizomai* does not appear in that verse. However, in verse twenty-eight Paul warns the Philippians of impending persecution. He teaches them that suffering is part of the Christian's earthly experience (v. 29) and then tells them, "Having the same *conflict* which ye saw in me, and now hear to be in me" (Phil. 1:30) [emphasis mine]. The word *conflict* is the same noun used in Hebrews 12:1. Jude uses the verb form for "earnestly contend" in Jude 3. Local churches must consistently proclaim the gospel and seek the salvation of the lost. They will face opposition and persecution in that evangelistic ministry. Proclaiming the gospel will be a struggle.

The spirit of militance of which the New Testament speaks is not a light thing. Believers stand together "for the faith of the gospel," and it will cost them. Paul was in prison for his faith and would eventually suffer a martyr's death. The Philippian believers also faced persecution (Phil. 1:28). In the face of opposition and persecution, we must view our commitment to the faith as a struggle. Because we possess "the faith" revealed from God, we contend for it at any cost.

Christianity is built on God's revelation. Positively, we contend for the Word of God. Negatively, we stand against those who pervert and deny it. Thus our ministry is a struggle. Scripture assures us that believers will suffer in contending for "the faith." Biblical militance is a sober, thought-out stand for the absolute truth of Scripture and against the false doctrine that denies the Word. It is not an arrogant "I know better" attitude. It is not a self-motivated stance that seeks to make a name for the crusader against evil. It is a commitment to

God's revelation. It disregards self and stands ready to pay any price in proclaiming truth.

The twentieth century has reportedly been the bloodiest century in human history. Millions of those who have lost their lives died martyr's deaths for "the faith." They were possessed of a militant spirit, wrought in the conviction that God's Word is absolute truth. Let us stand up for that truth and preach it boldly for the conversion of souls. Let us not surrender to the relativistic attitude of a prevailing culture. We who believe the Bible and obey its authority must develop a mindset. We must understand and accept the fact that we not only must affirm the Bible as God's revelation, *but we must be ready to pay any price in contending for that faith!*

Fighting for the Faith

Paul saw the ministry as a fight. He used Jude's word "contend" to exhort Timothy and to give his own testimony. He tells Timothy to "Fight the good fight of (the) faith" (I Tim. 6:12). He comes to the end of his own life and boldly reports, "I have fought a good fight, I have finished my course, I have kept the faith" (II Tim. 4:7). In each verse he uses the word for "contend," and in each verse he relates "the fight" to "the faith." We fight for the faith, or contend for it, when we boldly proclaim it and expose its enemies. Jude builds on Paul's attitude when he exhorts us to "earnestly contend for the faith." He is not alone when he urges a militant spirit upon present-day believers.

Resistance to Militance

New Evangelicalism

First generation New Evangelicals chafed under the militance of Fundamentalism and rejected it. Carl F. H. Henry's

1947 book, *The Uneasy Conscience of Modern Fundamentalism,* voiced this frustration. He clearly stated his thesis:

> Those who read with competence will know that the "uneasy conscience" of which I write is not one troubled about the great Biblical verities, which I consider the only outlook capable of resolving our problems, but rather one distressed by the frequent failure to apply them effectively to crucial problems confronting the modern mind.[5]

Harold John Ockenga, writing the introduction for Henry, complained about "Fundamentalist isolationism."[6] Henry himself analyzed Fundamentalism "in terms of an anti-ecumenical spirit of independent isolationism."[7] Ten years later Ockenga would follow the same theme, saying, "The New Evangelicalism is the application of historic Christianity to the social problems of our day."[8] Ockenga was really arguing for more social awareness from Christians. However, he pushed the envelope when he stated, "There need be no disagreement between the personal gospel and the social gospel."[9] He went on to announce "that the strategy of the New Evangelicalism has changed from one of separation to infiltration."[10]

---

[5]Carl F. H. Henry, *The Uneasy Conscience of Modern Fundamentalism* (Grand Rapids: Wm. B. Eerdmans Publishing Company, 1947), p. 11.

[6]Ibid., p. 13.

[7]Ibid., p. 19.

[8]Harold John Ockenga, Press Release, December 8, 1957, Boston, The Park Street Church.

[9]Ibid. With this statement Ockenga revealed that he had capitulated to the thinking of modernism in this area. The "social gospel" is the doctrine of Walter Rauschenbusch, developed from the teaching of Schleiermacher and Ritschl. It is the idea of redemption by improving man's physical condition. We must be fair and say that Ockenga was still orthodox in his theology, and believed in the necessity of the New Birth for people to be saved. Henry also makes that point repeatedly in *Uneasy Conscience.* Yet Ockenga deliberately used the term as a part of his attempt to pursue dialogue with Modernists and to infiltrate their ranks. *While the gospel of Christ affects society through the changed lives of those who are saved, there is no such thing as a social gospel in Scripture!*

[10]Ibid.

This strategic change has produced tragic results in Christianity in the last forty years.[11] Beginning as a theologically orthodox movement, the New Evangelicalism now includes a wide spectrum of doctrinal views. Most notable are the widely divergent views on the inerrancy of Scripture, the eternal destiny of man, and the nature of hell. Many New Evangelicals are even surrendering the integrity of the gospel itself through the "Evangelicals and Catholics Together" publications. Mark Sidwell notes the shift in New Evangelical thinking about the so-called social gospel. Originally, "Ockenga and Carl Henry sought a testimony on social issues that was based on the redemption of the individual through Christ."[12] Now many in the present generation "view social action as a form of evangelism rather than a means to evangelism," and some even "make social reform a part of the gospel itself."[13]

New Evangelicals wanted to maintain Fundamentalism's historic theological orthodoxy while rejecting its separatism and militance. The grand experiment proved to be a disaster.[14] The reason for the disaster appears simple to this observer. Both orthodoxy ("the faith which was once delivered") and militancy ("earnestly contend") are biblical concepts. One cannot be forsaken without causing harm to the other. Those who embrace God's revelation *must* "earnestly contend" for it.

---

[11]For a full discussion of the theological erosion in New Evangelicalism, see Ernest Pickering, *The Tragedy of Compromise* (Greenville, SC: Bob Jones University Press, 1994).

[12]Mark Sidwell, *The Dividing Line* (Greenville, SC: Bob Jones University Press, 1998), p. 117.

[13]Ibid.

[14]New Evangelicals have written extensively about their crisis. Some of the literature includes Michael Horton, ed., *The Agony of Deceit* (Chicago: Moody Press, 1990); Horton, *Made in America* (Grand Rapids: Baker Book House, 1991); David F. Wells, *No Place for Truth* (Grand Rapids: Wm. B. Eerdmans Publishing Company, 1993); and John H. Armstrong, ed., *The Coming Evangelical Crisis* (Chicago: Moody Press, 1996).

Restless Fundamentalists

It is striking to note that some younger Fundamentalists today are resisting the idea of militance. With ecumenical compromise, apostate denial of God's Word, and godlessness active on every hand, antipathy to militance among Fundamentalists is hard to comprehend.

Why Resist Militance?

David Doran cites several indications that some Fundamentalists resist the militancy of former years. He lists "a genuine loss of clarity among many about the very nature or meaning of Fundamentalism," "a loss of conviction among many Fundamentalists," and "the subtle, and sometimes open repudiation of speaking out about separatism."[15]

Douglas McLachlan provides insight into the reasoning of some who resist this idea of militance. He writes about "the element which I believe is most foundational to fundamentalism—the element of *absolute truth*" [emphasis McLachlan's].[16] McLachlan's statement supports our contention that truth revealed from God, which Jude calls "the faith," is the foundation of New Testament Christianity and of the Fundamentalist movement. McLachlan then states, "In historic, biblical fundamentalism you find not only belief in the fundamentals of the faith, but you find a readiness to support those fundamentals by a form of biblical separatism."[17] After defining separatism he comments,

> While this is a teaching which should be warmly supported by the people of God, it has lost some of its luster in this part of the 20th century due to a couple of responses which have served to tarnish it:

[15]David M. Doran, "In Defense of Militancy," *The Sentinel*, pp. 1-2.
[16]Douglas R. McLachlan, "Fundamentalism: What's in a Name?" (Central Baptist Theological Seminary, 1998, lecture notes), p. 2.
[17]Ibid., p. 3.

Dispositional Offensiveness. Unless we are extremely cautious, it is easy for us to take the shape of assaulting everybody who disagrees with us with the result that we end up projecting a very ugly disposition. Too often this looks much more like "the works of the flesh" than "the fruit of the Spirit" (Galatians 5:19-23). It is something which grieves the Holy Spirit.

Defective Lines. Unless we are committed to critical exegesis of the text of Scripture in its context, it becomes very easy for us to draw lines that are not anchored to Bible absolutes but personal preferences. New "qualifiers" which were not originally a part of the equation, and which are not sourced in Scripture, begin to reshape our definition of fundamentalism and unnecessarily alienate people from it.[18]

McLachlan, affirming Fundamentalism and the accompanying separatism, reports the reasons why some repudiate separatism and acknowledges that the allegations are not without some basis in reality.

David Burggraff also describes "an anti-militant attitude, the decline of the spirit of militancy."[19] He says,

Having grown up in the 1960s, which saw the revolt against absolute values, today's fundamentalists have been influenced by our culture which has held a general disdain for militancy on almost any subject. There is the dread of being thought of as too negative, combative.[20]

Doran sees the same issues as Burggraff and McLachlan:

Again, the negative impact of pastors/people who have strong convictions that are backed by non-biblical arguments (if any at all) has had its toll. But so has the generation's worth of relativism and pragmatism that has been

---

[18]Ibid., p. 4.
[19]David L. Burggraff, "What Will Keep Us from Becoming New, New Evangelicals?" (Calvary Baptist Seminary, n.d., unpublished paper), p. 5.
[20]Ibid.

pumped into our churches via our culture. Any dogmatism that claims to be biblical must certainly be backed by careful exegesis, and for this we must strive.[21]

The Need for a Right Spirit

The Bible commands separation from unbelief and teaches us we are in a battle with satanic and demonic forces of evil (II Cor. 6:14–7:1; Eph. 6:12; I Tim. 4:1). The New Testament writers used bold language in denouncing false teachers (Phil. 3:18, 19; II Tim. 2:17, 18; II Pet. 2; Jude 5-19). Militance is biblical!

We must note that Scripture also urges a right spirit upon those who "earnestly contend for the faith" (Jude 3). *A biblical disposition and ethical conduct are mandatory, along with biblical militance.* The Holy Spirit requires meekness and gentleness (II Cor. 10:1) as we take up the "weapons of our warfare" (II Cor. 10:4). Paul commands Timothy to "shun" false teaching, "depart from iniquity," "flee youthful lusts," "avoid" that which "genders strifes," and to "instruct" those who fall into this "iniquity." He declares that those who embrace error are in "the snare of the devil" (II Tim. 2:25, 26). That surely looks like a bold, militant opposition to false teaching. In the same passage Paul teaches Timothy not to wrangle, but rather to be gentle, able to teach, patient, and meek as he opposes and instructs "those that oppose themselves" (II Tim. 2:24, 25). Scripture commands and describes the godly spirit that complements militance for the Faith and against false doctrine.

Having said that, we must turn the equation around and say that **biblical militance is mandatory, along with a biblical spirit and ethical conduct!** Just as it is wrong to be militant with a combative spirit, so it is also wrong to exhibit a

---

[21]Doran, p. 1.

proper spirit without militance. No one should try to justify harsh and unethical conduct in the pursuit of militance. Neither should one try to justify forsaking militance because some have displayed a wrong spirit.[22]

Some have alleged a "mean streak" in Fundamentalism. This writer's opinion is that the so-called "mean streak" is not peculiar to Fundamentalists, but to human nature. Any believer not controlled by the Holy Spirit is capable of displaying a carnal spirit. Some in the New Evangelical camp have prominently displayed the same kind of spirit. Vernon Grounds led in the New Evangelical movement from its beginning. He fought against the separatists in the Conservative Baptist movement. His spirit when he wrote the following could rightly be questioned:

> Undeniably evangelicalism is fundamentalism, if by fundamentalism is meant a tenacious insistence upon the essential and central dogmas of historic Christianity. Yet just as undeniably evangelicalism is not fundamentalism as fundamentalism is ordinarily construed. A thoroughgoing evangelical recognizes with a wry smile the truth in the liberal jibe: "*Fundamentalism is too much fun, too much damn, and too little mental!*" [emphasis mine].[23]

In later years, Donald Carson, Carl Henry, and Kenneth Kantzer referred to the politics and infighting within New Evangelical circles.[24]

This in no way justifies any carnal display by a Fundamentalist, nor does it excuse any such conduct. It simply demonstrates that carnality is not a distinctive characteristic of Fundamentalism.

---

[22]For a detailed discussion of this subject see Fred Moritz, *Be Ye Holy: The Call to Christian Separation* (Greenville, SC: Bob Jones University Press, 1994), pp. 89-98.

[23]Vernon Grounds, "The Nature of Evangelicalism," *Eternity*, February 1956, p. 13.

[24]*Know Your Roots: Evangelicalism Yesterday, Today, and Tomorrow* (Madison: 2100 Productions, 1991), videocassette.

A Good Example

Fundamentalists *can* display a good spirit in the conflict. William Bell Riley preached at the first meeting of the Fundamental Fellowship in 1920. The Fundamental Fellowship within the Northern Baptist Convention met to raise a protest against the Modernism within the Convention. Riley addressed the meeting on the subject "Modernism in Baptist Schools."[25] Riley named various schools where modernism was rife. He called the names of men who were propounding modernism and denying the faith. His message was a hard-hitting address. Yet as he began, Riley displayed a gentlemanly, Christ-like spirit, saying,

> It could hardly be necessary for me, in the very outset of this address, to disclaim all disposition to offensive personalities. Some of the schools to which I refer, I have never seen; the most of the men whose names I shall call and from whose lips and pens I shall quote, are delightful, cultured gentlemen; to know them intimately is to be enamored of them. I love them!
>
> This discussion has to do wholly with opinions, not with personalities, and I propose to relate it to three themes: The Baptist Faith Defined, The Baptist Faith Denied, and the Baptist Denomination Endangered.[26]

The Need for Right Standards

McLachlan also cites "defective lines" as the second reason some resist militance. He is absolutely correct that "unless we are committed to critical exegesis of the text of Scripture in its context, it becomes very easy for us to draw lines that are not anchored to Bible absolutes but personal preferences."[27] Doran has said the same: "Any dogmatism that claims to be

---

[25]William Bell Riley, "Modernism in Baptist Schools" in *Baptist Fundamentals* (Philadelphia: The Judson Press, 1920), pp. 167-87.

[26]Ibid., p. 168.

[27]McLachlan, p. 4.

biblical must certainly be backed by careful exegesis, and for this we must strive."[28] We must note that Christians today face some issues to which Scripture does not expressly speak. However, we are responsible to base our actions on clear principles of Scripture that will apply to the situations we face.

By way of illustration, Scripture does not speak about film entertainment. However, Scripture does give the eternal principle that governs a believer's thought life. Philippians 4:8 declares,

> Finally, brethren, whatsoever things are true, whatsoever things are honest, whatsoever things are just, whatsoever things are pure, whatsoever things are lovely, whatsoever things are of good report; if there be any virtue, and if there be any praise, think on these things.

Though we have no express statements on film entertainment, we do have this principle from God that clearly rules out the immorality, immodesty, murder, other violence, profanity, and godlessness that dominate the movie industry, the television networks, the movie channels, the music channels, and much of the print media that reflect our culture. New Testament Christians who apply biblical standards to their lives and seek to glorify God are, by the very nature of the case, going to avoid this kind of sin and live counter to the culture of our world in many aspects of their lives.[29]

God's Word is revealed, or "delivered," truth (Jude 3). We accept it as absolute truth from our Creator. Our post-modern world is in total rebellion against absolute truth. Christians who live according to the absolute principles of the Bible will find themselves in conflict with the world system. Our Lord foretold that fact (John 16:33) and prayed for our purity as we live in this world (John 17:15-17). Jesus then promised that

---

[28]Doran, p. 1.

[29]For a fuller discussion see Moritz, pp. 35-42.

when believers live for Him in this world, others will believe and be saved (John 17:20). Living for Christ in a hostile culture requires courage, the power of God, and a militant spirit. That militant spirit is based on the conviction that God's Word is an absolute revelation. This kind of godly living gives the ministry and the individual life its distinctiveness. It makes the Christian "salt and light" (Matt. 5:13-16). It is the key to God's power and blessing.

A Warning

Modern Fundamentalists who question the concept of militance need to seriously consider any actions they take. No doubt some Fundamentalists have acted harshly and even unbiblically at times. Those who would forsake a militant spirit need to remember that *earnestly contending for revealed Scripture is biblical!* By all means, disavow a carnal and unbiblical spirit. But, by all means, display a biblical spirit with biblical militance. Do not forsake godly, biblical standards because you see some who take positions Scripture does not justify. Do not forsake a biblically militant spirit just because some have been unbiblically harsh. Too often we can react against one unbiblical extreme and end up embracing the opposite extreme instead of coming to a position taught by Scripture. We must not reject carnality and embrace compromise. To forsake biblical militance is to start down a slippery slope that will inevitably lead to disaster in theology, association, and practice. The New Evangelical movement has demonstrated that.

Conclusion

Wickedness abounds on every hand, and moral decay increases with alarming speed in our world. Men reveal the capabilities that lie within the depraved hearts of those without

Christ. The gospel is mankind's only hope. Bible believers need to contend for the faith and proclaim it and the Savior it reveals. False religion either denies God's Word or leads people into a self-centered mysticism by adding to that Word. Ecumenical evangelistic endeavors bring thousands together, obliterating the difference between true doctrine taught in the Scriptures and systems built on religious work. Theologians issue proclamations that attempt to wed justifying faith and sacramental grace. "The faith which was once delivered unto the saints" (Jude 3) stands against all this. It is nothing when liberals hurl epithets at us and New Evangelicals like Grounds repeat them with glee. We are neither anti-intellectual nor obscurantist. A God-hating, Scripture-rejecting world will always cast reproach upon us. God's truth merits our loyalty and obedience no matter what price we may pay. Now is not the time to give in to the prevailing relativism of our age. This is the time to "earnestly contend for the faith." We must stand distinct from and against the enemies of the cross.

THE FUNDAMENTALISTS' FOES

You have no enemies, you say?
Alas, my friend, the boast is poor;
He who has mingled in the fray
Of duty, that the brave endure,
Must have made foes! If you have none,
You've hit no traitor on the hip,
You've dashed no cup from perjured lip,
You've never turned the wrong to right,
You've been a coward in the fight.

– Charles Mackay

For there are certain men crept in unawares, who were before of old ordained to this condemnation, ungodly men, turning the grace of our God into lasciviousness, and denying the only Lord God, and our Lord Jesus Christ (Jude 4).

Jude now comes to the reason for his urgent epistle. "Certain men" have stealthily crept into the Christian community. They pose a deadly danger to the local churches. These men exhibit godlessness in their character and apostasy in their doctrine. Bible-believing Christians must enter into a battle for "the faith" (v. 3). True Christians must stand against these impostors.

Jude's call is as real today as when he wrote it. False teachers of the same character and advocating the same blasphemous teachings are busily at work today. As in Jude's day, they camouflage themselves under the guise of Christianity. Fundamentalist Christians must contend for the faith against these enemies.

The Enemies' Treachery

These enemies of the faith have conducted a subversive operation. They have "crept in unawares" (v. 4). M. R. Vincent states, "The verb means *to get in by the side,* to slip in by a side-door" [emphasis Vincent's].[1] Gordon Lovik comments: "By a literal translation it means they have put on a masquerade and have quietly come alongside, slipping into the company of believers."[2]

Their Judgment

Jude teaches that these false teachers are marked out for God's judgment. In later verses he describes the coming judgment that awaits these men. God has set a precedent. He has already judged rebellion. In accordance with His righteous and unchanging character, He will do it again. These impostors will be judged as God judged the unbelieving in Israel (v. 5). As fallen angels are now reserved to judgment (v. 6), so these false teachers will know the wrath of God. Sodom and Gomorrah stand as vivid examples of the righteous judgment of God (v. 7). These "filthy dreamers" (v. 8) are condemned to the same "vengeance of eternal fire" (v. 7).

Their Character

The Holy Spirit sums up these false teachers' character in one term—they are "ungodly men" (v. 4). In quoting Enoch Jude uses this term four more times in verse fifteen. He talks of "all that are ungodly among them," of their "ungodly deeds which they have ungodly committed," finally calling them "ungodly sinners." Lovik explains the full force of God's description of them:

---

[1]Marvin R. Vincent, *Word Studies in the New Testament* (1887; reprint, Grand Rapids: Wm. B. Eerdmans Publishing Company, 1989), I:713.

[2]Gordon H. Lovik, *"These Men" in Your Church* (Minneapolis: Central C. B. Seminary, n.d.), p. 25.

These men are further classified as ungodly. They are not atheistic, but *asebeis*, that is, they have a complete disregard and defiance toward God's person. They do not reject the reality of the existence of God, but they refuse to humble themselves before Him.[3]

The Enemies' Tactics

Jude exposes the false teachers of whom he writes in two ways. He describes the error of their practice and the error of their doctrine. Contrary to how we might do it, he speaks of their practice before he denounces their theology.

Promoting Lasciviousness

Jude rebukes their practice by saying they turn "the grace of our God into lasciviousness" (v. 4). This "turning" is a transposition, or a transfer.[4] They replace God's grace with license. The English "lasciviousness" represents the Greek word *aselgia*. This strong word, used several times in the New Testament, refers to "debauchery."[5] The word describes Sodom and Gomorrah (II Pet. 2:7) and the world without God (Eph. 4:19), and in several places it refers specifically to sexual sins.[6] Bauerenfeind goes on to say, "man naturally falls victim to this when cut off from God."[7] All men, separated from God by willful sin, are capable of lasciviousness (Eph. 4:18, 19). As the false teachers Jude describes deliberately rebel against God, it is no wonder they live in such a debauched, lascivious

[3]Lovik, pp. 30-31.

[4]Joseph Henry Thayer, *Greek-English Lexicon of the New Testament* (Grand Rapids: Zondervan Publishing House, 1962 edition), p. 406.

[5]Otto Bauerenfeind, "aselgia" in Gerhard Kittel, ed., *Theological Dictionary of the New Testament* (Grand Rapids: Wm. B. Eerdmans Publishing Company, 1964), I:490.

[6]Ibid.

[7]Ibid.

way (II Pet. 2:7). It should come as no surprise that these false teachers advocate this kind of a lifestyle in those they lead.

Previous Warnings of Lasciviousness

Jude's caution comes at the end of a long history of New Testament warnings concerning indecent and dissolute conduct. Many commentators write extensively of the parallel between Peter's warnings in II Peter 2 and those in Jude's epistle. Apparently, Paul spoke of the same danger of which Jude warned, saying, "What shall we say then? Shall we continue in sin, that grace may abound?" (Rom. 6:1). Barnes notes, "The liability of the doctrines of grace to be thus abused was foreseen by Paul, and against such abuse he earnestly sought to guard the Christians of his time."[8] Paul seems to warn the Galatian churches in a similar fashion, saying, "For, brethren, ye have been called unto liberty; only use not liberty for an occasion to the flesh, but by love serve one another" (Gal. 5:13). This exhortation precedes his warning against the "works of the flesh" (Gal. 5:19-21), and lasciviousness is one of those fleshly products.

As previously noted, Paul also uses the word in Ephesians 4:19. Ephesus was a city completely given to ungodly living. The city worshiped Diana, the goddess of fertility, as its patron. In 1970 my wife and I saw the ruins of the old buildings we would today call casinos, with the wine bowls sculpted into the floors and gambling games carved on their surfaces. Marble pavement preserves the ancient versions of billboards at the street corners, showing directions to nearby houses of prostitution. The apostle's readers certainly understood Paul's emphasis when he wrote that the Gentile culture had dedicated itself to debauchery (Eph. 4:18, 19). He did not merely condemn the sins of the ungodly Ephesian culture, but also

---

[8]Albert Barnes, *Notes on the New Testament: James, Peter, John, and Jude* (1848; reprint, Grand Rapids: Baker Book House, 1979), p. 390.

instructed the believers to "walk not as other Gentiles walk, in the vanity of their mind" (Eph. 4:17).

The idea that God's grace releases believers to live any way they wish is an old heresy. Paul saw the danger and warned Christians not to fall into such error. Jude exposed those who propounded this heresy. He described both the proponents of this doctrine and their practice as "ungodly" (Jude 4, 15). This unbiblical and ungodly transposition of grace into lasciviousness is nothing more than wicked justification for self-centered gratification.

The Biblical Antidote

Scripture clearly identifies the false teachers and their unrestrained lifestyles. Scripture also warns believers against this danger. But Scripture does not leave Christians in a spiritual vacuum with no teaching on *how* to avoid such debauchery. The Bible teaches Christians that the same grace that saves them and frees them from the bondage of the law also provides them the possibility of victory over sin. Paul says,

> For the grace of God that bringeth salvation hath appeared to all men, *Teaching* us that denying ungodliness and worldly lusts, we should live soberly, righteously, and godly, in this present world; Looking for that blessed hope, and the glorious appearing of the great God and our Savior Jesus Christ; Who gave himself for us, that he might redeem us from all iniquity, and purify unto himself a peculiar people, zealous of good works (Tit. 2:11-14) [emphasis mine].

The key to this passage is the word *teaching* (v. 12). In his classic little work, Christian layman J. F. Strombeck declared that "the very same grace which brings salvation also teaches the saved how to live 'godly in this present world.' "[9] In simple language, Strombeck precisely described the biblical teaching:

---

[9] J. F. Strombeck, *Disciplined by Grace: Studies in Christian Conduct* (Moline, IL: Strombeck Foundation, 1975), pp. 8-9.

In the above passage, this teaching work of grace is emphasized. In the original text the meaning is: "to train up a child, to chasten, to instruct, to teach." The same word in Hebrews 12:6, 7 and 10 is translated by some form of the word chasten. Thus when grace teaches, it does more than impart knowledge as an instructor. It teaches in the sense that wise parents train and discipline children.[10]

Grace that saves from sin also teaches the saved to deny the wickedness of sin in modern-day culture. To say it another way, God gives the gift of *saving grace,* and He also gives the gift of *sanctifying grace.* His grace does not justify self-centered gratification; rather, it disciplines the believer to deny ungodly desires and live righteously. Any teaching that neglects or *minimizes* the grace of God as it applies to victorious living perverts what God's Word teaches about true grace.[11]

The Enemies' Teaching

"These men" (Jude 4, 8, 10, 12, 16, 19) infiltrate New Testament churches. They also teach and practice a lifestyle that perverts God's grace. Jude's final warning concerning them is that they "deny the only Lord God, and our Lord Jesus Christ." Bible scholars debate the meaning of this statement. The issue is whether the statement refers to God the Father and the Lord Jesus, or whether Jude uses both phrases to refer to Christ. We cannot go into the question in detail, but our position is that both phrases refer to Christ. We hold this because (1) Jude already refers to the Father ("the grace of our God"), and (2) Peter uses nearly identical language to refer to our Savior (II Pet. 2:1). The lordship of Christ is the point of controversy with apostates.

---

[10]Ibid., p. 9.

[11]Mark Sidwell, *The Dividing Line* (Greenville, SC: Bob Jones University Press, 1998), p. 19, has an eloquent statement on the issue of holiness and the world. His assertion is that "the character of the world is not morally neutral."

The Meaning of Lordship

Jude reports that these subverters of the faith deny "the only Lord God, and our Lord Jesus Christ" (v. 4). He uses two separate words, each of which is translated "Lord." The second word for "Lord" is the word *kurion*, which means "lord, master."[12] Among other uses, the New Testament uses the word as a title for Jesus Christ.

The first word Jude uses for "Lord" is *despotes*. The New Testament uses this word only ten times.[13] *Despotes* appears in our English language as "despot." It conveys a pejorative meaning, describing totalitarian dictators. It came to be used that way in Greek, but originally (and in this passage) carried a fuller meaning. It refers to Christ's "absolute, unrestricted power."[14] It can be used of a slave owner (I Tim. 6:1) or of the master of a house (II Tim. 2:21). In the latter case, it illustrates Christ's authority over the believer. Simeon used the word in addressing God. In Luke 2:29, after seeing the baby Jesus, he said, "Lord, now lettest thou thy servant depart in peace, according to thy word." God had promised him that he would not see death until he had seen the Messiah. Having seen the babe, and recognizing that God as despotes held absolute control of his life, he surrendered to God's will for his passage to the glory. God is Lord, even of our days.

[12]William F. Arndt and F. Wilbur Gingrich, *A Greek-English Lexicon of the New Testament* (Chicago: University of Chicago Press, 1957), p. 459.

[13]Karl Heinrich Rengstorf, "δεσπότης" in Gerhard Kittel, ed., *Theological Dictionary of the New Testament* (Grand Rapids: Wm. B. Eerdmans Publishing Company, 1964), II:49.

[14]R.C.H. Lenski, *The Interpretation of I and II Epistles of Peter, the Three Epistles of John, and the Epistle of Jude* (Minneapolis: Augsburg Publishing House, 1966), p. 305.

Jesus Is Lord

Peter and Jude use the word *despotes* to speak of the Lord Jesus Christ. When used of Jesus, it underscores His authority. Christ, who shed His blood to provide salvation for even those who deny Him (II Pet. 2:1), is Lord. He has the right to absolute power over His people. As the risen Lord He claimed that power (Matt. 28:18). Peter and Jude declare that false teachers deny Jesus Christ because of their self-willed, rebellious refusal to bow to His lordship. Christ is the eternally existent Son of God, who was born of a virgin. Scripture reveals that He lived a sinless life, died a substitutionary death for the ungodly, rose bodily from the grave, and ascended to Heaven. The Bible further promises that He will come again. These truths are vital to New Testament Christianity, and all true believers will acknowledge them. They also establish the lordship of Christ. Born-again Christians will reveal the fruit of their salvation in a godly lifestyle, and they will live under Christ's authority.

What It All Means

Jude established that New Testament Christianity was beset with impostors who infiltrated local churches. These ungodly impostors brought a wicked lifestyle and false doctrine into the churches. Jude exposed these men when he urged first-century believers to "earnestly contend for the faith" (Jude 3). This background offers present-day Christians several conclusions and applications.

Related Errors

The twin heresies of these who "slip in by the side-door" are not disjointed, but rather fit together. The fact that these men came into the churches with the two particular errors of lascivious living and denial of Christ's lordship was not coincidental. They share a common denominator. That common denominator is the nature of sin. *Self* lies at the heart of each of their attacks on New Testament Christianity. Augustus Hopkins Strong provides keen insight into the essence of sin:

> We hold the essential principle of sin to be selfishness. By selfishness we mean not simply the exaggerated self-love which constitutes the antithesis of benevolence, but that choice of self as the supreme end which constitutes the antithesis of supreme love to God.[15]

Scripture proves Strong's thesis. First, when Satan sinned, he declared his rebellion with five statements against God. In each statement, beginning with the words "I will" (Isa. 14:13, 14), Satan placed his self-will in diametric opposition to God's will. Second, the Bible shows that Eve's sin was a three-fold decision of her self-will. She saw that the fruit of the tree would satisfy her desires ("good for food"), please her ("pleasant to the eyes"), and advance her own interest ("desired to make one wise") (Gen. 3:6). We can almost hear her ask Satan, "What is in it for me?" Again, we can almost hear her decide, "I can gain something by disobedience to God that I will never have if I obey Him." Third, when rebellious men refuse to glorify God, who has revealed Himself to them in the creation, they change "the glory of the uncorruptible God into an image made like to corruptible man" (Rom. 1:23). Man attempts to make himself his own God. Fourth, Paul teaches that the violence and wickedness of the last days will occur because "men shall be lovers of their own selves" (II Tim. 3:2). Scripture clearly teaches that selfishness is truly the essence of sin.

This fact obviously relates to Jude's exposure of the enemies of the faith. Lasciviousness is debauched, unrestrained living, whether sexual or otherwise. Sinful men who live

---

[15]Augustus Hopkins Strong, *Systematic Theology* (Valley Forge, PA: The Judson Press, 1907), p. 567.

without restraint grasp for all the self-gratification they can seize. Theologically, the reason for denying the Bible's teaching about Christ is so that men will not have to acknowledge and submit to His authority. Selfishness is the fuel that runs the engine of man's sinfulness.

We who are saved by faith in Christ must recognize the deadly danger of self. Christians must decide with Paul "that they which live *should not henceforth live unto themselves*, but unto him which died for them and rose again" (II Cor. 5:15) [emphasis mine].

The Present Situation

The parallel between first-century Christianity and the present day is striking. God's Word is as up to date as today's newspaper or television newscast (or more so!). In the introduction of this book, we noted George Marsden's description of Fundamentalism. Note again how he drew the comparison in early Fundamentalism between apostate doctrine and godless conduct:

> Briefly, it [Fundamentalism] was militantly anti-modernist Protestant evangelicalism. Fundamentalists were evangelical Christians . . . who in the twentieth century militantly opposed both modernism in theology *and the cultural changes that modernism endorsed.* Militant opposition to modernism was what most clearly set off fundamentalism from a number of closely related traditions. . . [emphasis mine].[16]

Marsden recognizes that the early Fundamentalists saw the relationship between doctrine and lifestyle. Rejection of God's truth in either area of life grows out of selfishness. Further, men deny the idea of a God who gives absolute rules for human conduct in the Ten Commandments and before whom

---

[16]George Marsden, *Fundamentalism and American Culture* (Oxford: Oxford University Press, 1980), p. 4.

they will one day stand in judgment. Thus, they are free to live as they will.

> In vain they call old notions "fudge,"
> And bend their conscience to their doing.
> The Ten Commandments will not budge,
> And stealing still is stealing.[17]

This philosophy must inevitably ruin lives and the culture in which men live. Modern-day Fundamentalists must fight the same enemies that Jude and the Fundamentalists of the earlier parts of the twentieth century fought.

New Evangelical Capitulation

David Wells created a firestorm when he wrote his 1993 volume titled No Place for Truth. He describes the self-centered character of modern culture, saying,

> Western culture once valued the higher achievements of human nature—reasoned discourse, the good use of language, fair and impartial law, the importance of our collective memory, tradition, the core of moral axioms to which collective consent was given, those aesthetic achievements in the arts that represented the high-water marks of the human spirit. These are now all in retreat. Reasoned discourse has largely disappeared; in a nation of plummeting literacy, language has been reduced to the lowest common denominator, to the vulgar catch phrases of the youth culture; the core of values has disintegrated; the arts are degraded; the law is politicized; politics is trivialized. In place of high culture we have what is low. Unruly instinctual drives replace thought; the darker side of human nature destroys the nobler, leaving a trail of pornography, violence, and indifference.[18]

---

[17]Author unknown. Dr. Richard V. Clearwaters often quoted this verse.
[18]David F. Wells, No Place for Truth, or Whatever Happened to Evangelical Theology? (Grand Rapids: Wm. B. Eerdmans Publishing Company, 1993), p. 169.

Wells describes the modern culture in language consistent with Jude's term "lasciviousness" and charges some within the Evangelical movement with surrender to its self-willed decadence.

> What is now in place is not exactly an alternative system of belief. What is in place is no system of belief at all. It is more like a vacuum into the quiet emptiness of which the self is reaching for meaning—and finding only itself. . . . Its essence is not right doctrine, values and behavior; its essence is the freedom to have no doctrines, no values, to be free to follow the stream of instinct that flows from the self wherever it may lead, *a point that the evangelical apologists for this approach advocate quite unabashedly and unselfconsciously* [emphasis mine].[19]

One cannot ignore the authority of Scripture without paying a fearsome price. The world will always be the enemy of God's people (John 16:33). Christians must not capitulate to the deceitful attractions of the world system. God's people are called to overcome the world and to love their God supremely (I John 2:13-17).

Standing Against the Advocates of Lasciviousness

It is critical that present-day Fundamentalists boldly preach God's Word against lascivious living, following the pattern Paul gave (Eph. 4:17-32). Several observers note that Fundamentalism is changing at this point. David Burggraff says it clearly:

> Separation for early fourth-phase separatist fundamentalism went hand in hand with the movement's interpretation of personal holiness. Holiness implies a complete separation from evil, which was taken to include all "worldly amusements" such as card playing, dancing, attendance at the cinema, and drinking. In recent years, however, suspicion of "the world" has dissipated consider-

---

[19]Ibid., pp. 169-70.

ably. The antipathy toward the broader culture so characteristic of fundamentalists in the forties through the early eighties has given way to ambivalence and the down-play of separation.[20]

Personal separation in practice grows from a Christian's understanding of God's holiness. Similarly, lasciviousness in practice grows out of the denial of Christ's deity and lordship. Today's Fundamentalist preachers must declare God's holiness and urge believers to imitate it in their lifestyles (I Pet. 1:15, 16). Fundamentalists can look to former generations for historical example. Far more importantly, they must look to Scripture and obey its mandate. God's Word *is* a revelation that God gave us once for all. Fundamentalists heartily believe and affirm that truth. We must then preach the holiness of life and the glorious Lord of that mighty revelation. When we live this truth, lifestyle issues will fall into alignment with God's Word. Card playing still boasts its old sinful origin, dancing is more sensual and suggestive than ever, and Hollywood entertainment grows ever more corrupt. Politicians and the pope condemn the film industry, while Christians rent the videos and watch the broadcast channels, seemingly without conscience. "Wine is," still, "a mocker," and "strong drink is raging: and whosoever is deceived thereby is not wise" (Prov. 20:1). Clothing styles change over centuries, but the changeless Word of God still teaches principles for appropriate dress (I Tim. 2:9). God's purpose for us is not to reform a godless culture, but to gather out "a people for his name" (Acts 15:14).

The people of God must be challenged to "shine as lights in the world" (Phil. 2:15). We must stand against the world system out of which God called us. We must fix our love on the God who called us out of that world system (I John 2:15-17).

---

[20]David L. Burggraff (Calvary Baptist Seminary, Lansdale, PA, lecture notes), p. 58.

Wells incisively describes worldliness as "that system of values which in any culture has the fallen sinner at its center, which takes no account of God or His Word, and which therefore views sin as normal and righteousness as abnormal."[21] Those who advocate godlessness in living are as much the foes of the faith as are those who deny the deity and lordship of Christ.

It Is Happening Today!

As I write this chapter, a good Christian friend has provided a dramatic illustration of "turning the grace of our God into lasciviousness" (Jude 4). That this passes for religion of any description should shock every believer, as it did my friend Bob.

> As Camilla Ballard waits in the darkness for a movie to begin, she asks herself one question. "Where am I going to find God in this film?" In L.A. Confidential she had to look past profanity, sex and violence for a glimpse of the Almighty. But she did find it—in the unconditional love of a prostitute played by Kim Basinger.
>
> "When her policeman-lover beats her up, she just takes it. What a picture of God!" said the youth director at First Presbyterian Church of Dallas. "And in the police officer"—who misjudges her earlier actions—"what a picture of ourselves. We just rail at God and beat him up, and he takes it because he understands the big picture."
>
> "Oh my gosh, I was just so excited. I thought about it for days."
>
> Ms. Ballard is among a growing number of religious people who advocate going to the movies for what Baptist layman Bruce Ruggles calls "an experience of worship." He doesn't often find the taste of eternity he seeks, says Mr. Ruggles, but when he does, the experience can bring tears to his eyes. Like other similarly minded Christians, Mr. Ruggles says he doesn't rate films by the movie codes

---

[21]Wells, p. 215.

for violence and sex. He rates them by his own code for their "ability to move me, to touch my humanity."[22]

This lengthy article verifies that these leaders are not alone. Another reveals the twisted thinking that can lead a so-called "minister" to such conclusions:

> Christians who love movies despite—and sometimes because of—the films' often "unGodly" themes base their defense of Hollywood's art partly on the idea that God can be found in every situation.
>
> "John Calvin said all of life is holy," said Brent Barry, director of adult ministries for Dallas' First Presbyterian Church. "If people can find God in movies, then they can begin to reflect in the same way in their lives."[23]

The article goes on for pages, describing how some churches are using movie clips in Sunday services and how other pastors, professors, and religious editors promote the use of movies.

A Response

This kind of perverted thinking demands a response. It appears that those who "crept in unawares" (Jude 4) have taken over leadership in some religious circles. The Word of God speaks to this kind of thinking in several ways. *First, Scripture categorically condemns the violence, profanity, and immorality that these "false prophets" who produce "evil fruit" (Matt. 7:15-18) promote!* Many biblical passages address the issue, but one is sufficient for our present argument:

> But fornication, and all uncleanness, or covetousness, **let it not be once named among you,** as becometh saints; Neither filthiness, nor foolish talking, nor jesting, which are not convenient: but rather giving of thanks. For this

---

[22]Christine Wicker, "Even R-Rated Films Suggest Redeeming Messages to Believers With Eyes to See" (Dallas: *The Dallas Morning News*, June 6, 1998), p. 1G.
[23]Ibid.

ye know, that no whoremonger, nor unclean person, nor covetous man, who is an idolater, hath any inheritance in the kingdom of Christ and of God. *Let no man deceive you with vain words:* for because of these things cometh the wrath of God upon the children of disobedience (Eph. 5:3-6) [emphasis mine].

No one can mistake Paul. Believers are not even to name, much less watch or practice the moral corruption that Hollywood produces and these people advocate watching. Any believer who follows this line of reasoning is deceived, and the "false prophet" who reasons thus is a deceiver.

Second, this twisted reasoning openly demonstrates the self-willed nature of sin. Note again the Baptist layman's aim: "Mr. Ruggles says he doesn't rate films by the movie codes for violence and sex. He rates them by his own code for their 'ability to move me, to touch my humanity.' "[24] This Baptist pretender has set aside the authority of the Word of God (of which Chester Tulga said, "The basic tenet of the historic Baptist faith is that the Bible is the Word of God and the sole authority of faith and practice")[25] and has gone looking for *what moves him!* This is a textbook illustration of self-will opposing God's revealed will. This thinking fits the model Paul described in Romans 1:21-24. Man refuses to glorify God and imposes himself in God's rightful place.

Third, this thinking blatantly admits its own wicked character, even using the language with which God condemns it in His Word! It is absolutely amazing to see one attempt to defend the "ungodly" themes of Hollywood as having any spiritual value. We have already seen that Jude uses that very term five times to describe the false teachers against whom he writes and their work (Jude 4, 15). As a mere sidebar, one can only smile sadly

---

[24]Ibid.

[25]Chester E. Tulga, "What Baptists Believe About Soul Liberty," *The Baptist Challenge* (Little Rock, AR: Central Baptist Church, October 1997), p. 21.

and wonder how John Calvin would react to seeing his teaching used in this way.

Standing Against the Apostates

Fundamentalists have generally done a good job of withstanding the theological attacks that God's enemies advanced. We must constantly renew our determination to be biblically militant. We must resolutely determine to maintain consistent separation from unbelief. Fundamentalists must continue to reject the blasphemies of so-called "bishops" who deny the resurrection of Christ. Likewise, we must continue to shun the conclusions of the New Testament "scholars" who have decided Jesus did not say what He said. Fundamentalists have been joined by a significant segment of the New Evangelical movement in opposing the sellout of the gospel in the Evangelicals and Catholics Together pronouncements. Fundamentalists largely identify and avoid the ecumenism of popular movements like Promise Keepers. We must continue our vigilance as we mark and avoid the enemies of the faith.

Fighting on Two Fronts

Christianity's enemies mount a two-pronged attack. They attack the faith on selfish moral grounds, seeking base self-gratification. They also attack the faith on rebellious theological grounds, hating to surrender self-will to the lordship of Christ. Fundamentalists have no choice but to counter both attacks. If we maintain our doctrinal integrity and at the same time surrender our moral purity, we will lose the battle.

Fundamentalist doctrine is rooted in God's revelation. We must make sure our standards for godly living also grow out of careful exegesis and application of Scripture. Fundamentalists must not be contentious, but at the same time they do not have to look for conflict. Those who promote lasciviousness and deny Christ's lordship are all around.

In Isaiah 28 God promises to meet the needs of His faithful people who live for Him when wickedness prevails. Isaiah writes,

> In that day shall the Lord of hosts be for a crown of glory, and for a diadem of beauty, unto the residue of his people, And for a spirit of judgment to him that sitteth in judgment, and for strength to them that turn the battle to the gate (Isa. 28:5, 6).

God's people are not on the defensive. God promises strength "to those who repulse an enemy, and drive him back to his own city's gate."[26] Jesus made a similar promise to His church, saying, "And I say also unto thee, That thou art Peter, and upon this rock I will build my church; and the gates of hell shall not prevail against it" (Matt. 16:18). We must not wage this war in our own strength, but in God's promised power. Claiming that promise of power and Christ's promise of victory, let us face the enemies of the faith and drive them back to the very gates of hell.

---

[26]George Rawlinson, "Isaiah," in H.D.M. Spence and Joseph S. Exell, eds., *The Pulpit Commentary* (New York: Funk and Wagnalls Company, 1909), I:448.

THE FUNDAMENTALISTS' FOCUS

Set my heart, O dear Father,
On Thee, and Thee only,
Give me a thirst for Thy presence divine.
Lord, keep my focus on loving Thee wholly,
Purge me from earth; Turn my heart after Thine.

A passion for Thee;
O Lord, set a fire in my soul, and a thirst for my
*   God.*
Hear Thou my prayer, Lord, Thy power impart.
Not just to serve, but to love Thee with all of my
*   heart* [1]

But ye, beloved, building up yourselves on your most holy
faith, praying in the Holy Ghost, *Keep yourselves in the*
love of God, looking for the mercy of our Lord Jesus Christ
unto eternal life (Jude 20-21) [emphasis mine].

In exhorting believers to "earnestly contend for the
faith," Jude pursues two trains of thought. He describes the
essence of genuine New Testament Christianity and also exposes the subversive false teachers who pervert it. Our purpose is strictly to understand his description of New
Testament Christianity and to see how it parallels Fundamentalism.

Jude's tone now changes as he describes genuine Christianity. He has described "the faith which was once delivered
unto the saints" and exhorted Christians to "earnestly contend" for it. He has also warned of the ungodly men who have
slipped into the churches with their godless living and their
denial of Christ (v. 4). After he denounces these enemies of

---

[1]Joe Zichterman, "A Passion for Thee" in *We're Singing*, 6th ed. (Taylors, SC: The Wilds Christian Association, Inc., 1997), p. 66. Used by permission.

the faith (vv. 4-19), he turns again to his Christian brethren. He pens final commands and encouragement to the local churches. These instructions, when followed, enable true believers to avoid the pitfalls of debauchery and apostasy that the infiltrators promote. His first exhortation is a simple statement. He commands believers, "Keep yourselves in the love of God" (v. 21).

A Consistent Exhortation

It is important to note that Jude's instruction to Christians is consistent with other New Testament passages that deal with apostasy. Jesus began the Olivet Discourse with warnings about false Christs (Matt. 24:4, 5), persecutions (Matt. 24:9), and false prophets (Matt. 24:11). He then warned His disciples, "And because iniquity shall abound, the love of many shall wax cold" (Matt. 24:12).

Paul warned Timothy of the dangerous, ungodly conditions of the last days and of the persecution of Christians that would accompany them (II Tim. 3:1-13). He closed the chapter by urging Timothy to continue in faithfulness to the gospel and to the instruction in the Word of God (II Tim. 3:14-17).

Peter spends two chapters of his second epistle warning of the false teachers and wicked conditions of the last days. In chapter 2 he takes the time to tell Christians they can be overcome by the sinfulness of the age, as was Lot, or they can have victory over temptation in God's power (II Pet. 2:7-9). In chapter 3 Peter urges believers who face the godlessness of the last days to be steadfast and to grow in grace (II Pet. 3:11-18).

So Jude's words are not unusual. They fit the Holy Spirit's pattern of warning and encouraging believers while denouncing the godlessness of the last days.

A Commanded Exhortation

To this point, Jude has emphasized the theological nature of New Testament faith. God reveals Himself to men in His Word. Christians must earnestly contend for that faith and stand against those who pervert God's grace and deny God's Son. But that is not all there is to Bible Christianity. New Testament Christianity also demands an intimate walk with the Lord. Jude stresses the importance of this walk with God by phrasing this exhortation—"Keep yourselves in the love of God"—as an imperative. Fellowship with God is not an addendum to Christian faith and life; it is an imperative. Christians will not please God and be all He wants them to be unless they maintain their love relationship with Him.

The Meaning of God's Love

In order to obey this command, we need to understand its meaning. Does Jude mean we are to maintain our love for God, or does he intend that we should keep ourselves in a relationship with Him so that we revel in His love for us? The latter seems to be true. Alford states that the emphasis is on God's love.[2] Lenski states, "To keep oneself in God's love is to stay where God can love us as his children and can shower upon us all the gifts of love that he has for those who are his children."[3] This statement is consistent with Jesus' words to the Twelve in the upper room. He charged them, "As the Father hath loved me, so have I loved you: continue ye in my love. If ye keep my commandments, ye shall abide in my love; even as I have kept my Father's commandments, and abide in

[2]Henry Alford, *The Greek Testament* (London: Rivingtons and Cambridge: Deighton, Bell, and Co., 1862), IV:541.

[3]R.C.H. Lenski, *The Interpretation of I and II Epistles of Peter, the Three Epistles of John, and the Epistle of Jude* (Minneapolis: Augsburg Publishing House, 1966), p. 646.

His love" (John 15:9, 10). New Testament Christians will properly crave fellowship with the Lord and desire to be assured of His love for them. This is a "great life-long act to be accomplished"[4] by believers.

The Impact of Keeping in God's Love

Scripture teaches that when Christians keep themselves in a relationship to God in which they are conscious of God's love for them, their lives will be affected in several ways.

Responding to God's Love

When we are properly aware of God's love, we will respond to that love. John the Apostle speaks of this in I John 4. He develops the theme that God is love and He demonstrated His love by sending Christ to be the Savior of men (I John 4:7-10). He then applies the truth of God's love to Christians in three ways. First, because God loves us, we should love our brethren in Christ (I John 4:11). Second, God's love for us gives us assurance (I John 4:17-18). Third, because God loves us, we respond to Him with our love. He says, "We love him, because he first loved us" (I John 4:19). Our natural response to God's love for us will be love for God.

The Results of Loving God

Keeping ourselves in the love of God will produce love for God in the lives of Christians. This love for God produces several direct results in the Christian's life. These results of loving God are vital to the Christian life and must be listed here.

First, loving God is our greatest duty as Christians. Moses instructed the nation of Israel concerning this, saying, "Hear,

---

[4]Alford, IV:541.

O Israel: The Lord our God is one Lord: And thou shalt love the Lord thy God with all thine heart, and with all thy soul, and with all thy might" (Deut. 6:4, 5). The Lord Jesus reiterated the importance of that great command. When asked "Master, which is the great commandment in the law?" (Matt. 22:36), Christ responded, "Thou shalt love the Lord thy God with all thy heart, and with all thy soul, and with all thy mind. This is the first and greatest commandment" (Matt. 22:37-38). Christians fulfill their first duty to God when they respond to the great love of God for them with their love for Him.

Second, the Christian's love for God is the key to obedience. God does not motivate believers to obey Him out of fear, but rather out of love for Him. This theme weaves its way consistently through Scripture. In the second of the Ten Commandments, God forbids idolatry. He gives His reason for forbidding it by saying,

> For I the Lord thy God am a jealous God, visiting the iniquity of the fathers upon the children unto the third and fourth generation of them that hate me; And showing mercy unto thousands of them that love me, and keep my commandments (Exod. 20:5, 6).

Jesus also appealed to one motive—our love for Him—when He asked for our obedience to the Word. He simply said, "If ye love me, keep my commandments" (John 14:15).

Third, the Christian's love for God is the basis upon which we will forsake sin and live for Christ. Simply put, personal separation from the world is an issue of our love for God! John states this in clear language: "Love not the world, neither the things that are in the world. If any man love the world, the love of the Father is not in him" (I John 2:15). The Christian who loves the philosophy and practices of this godless world system has a problem. Scripture identifies that problem with laserlike accuracy. The Christian who loves the world has grown cold in his love for his Father.

Fourth, the Christian's love for God will condition his attitude toward the material things of life. Jesus emphasized this in the Sermon on the Mount: "No man can serve two masters: for either he will hate the one, and love the other; or else he will hold to the one, and despise the other. Ye cannot serve God and mammon" (Matt. 6:24). The New Testament repeatedly warns Christians against the subtle evils of a materialistic spirit (e.g., I Cor. 5:10; Eph. 4:19; 5:3, 5). Paul clearly states that God warns believers against the will to be rich; that is, a covetous spirit. That kind of spirit sets up the Christian for great trouble (I Tim. 6:9-10). Clearly, the possession of wealth is not sin, for Paul in the same chapter gives direct instructions to believers who are rich (I Tim. 6:17-19). A covetous spirit shifts our trust and reliance from the living God to temporal things (I Tim. 6:17). That is sin. Moreover, the right attitude of every Christian toward material things, regardless of how much he has, depends on his love for God.

Fifth, the believer's love for God forms the basis for the call to Christian ministry. When Jesus reclaimed the backslidden Peter, He asked him the same question three times. The question was "Simon, son of Jonas, lovest thou me?" (John 21:15-17). When Peter averred his love for Christ, Jesus called him to "Feed my lambs" or "Feed my sheep" (John 21:15-17). Christ commissioned Peter to serve Him and told him that he would suffer a martyr's death (John 21:18). Though he had previously failed and denied his Lord (John 18:25-27), his love for Christ would now keep him faithful to that end.

Sixth, the converse is also true. A love for the things of the world is the reason some servants of Christ quit their Christian service. Paul sadly reports to Timothy that "Demas hath forsaken me, having loved this present world" (II Tim.

4:10). Though Demas is listed twice as one of Paul's faithful coworkers (Col. 4:14; Philem. 24), he has now left the ministry Paul reports. The reason for his failure was love for the world. Perhaps he was cowed by the threat of Paul's impending death. Whatever the cause, his love for the world caused him to leave the work. It is a tragedy when a preacher fails morally. It is no less a tragedy when opposition in the work, desire for material comfort, or some other worldly attitude drives a preacher from his God-given work. Whatever difficulties we may face will never exceed the terrible obstacles the apostles and countless others faced in the ministry. All disciples of Christ must be willing to deny themselves, take up the cross daily, and follow Jesus (Luke 9:23). The issue of "stick-to-it-iveness" in the ministry is an issue of love for Christ versus love for the world.

The Importance of Keeping in God's Love

This background shows us the vital importance of keeping ourselves in the love of God. When we as believers keep ourselves in the place where we are conscious of His love for us, we will respond to His love by loving Him. That love for God will keep us in fellowship with God as we obey the great commandment to love Him, obey His Word, separate from the wickedness of the world, build a right attitude toward material things, and serve Him faithfully. All this that comes out of our love for God is conditioned on our keeping ourselves in His love. Thus Jude's command to Christians goes to the heart of our success in the Christian life and fellowship with God.

A Practical Exhortation

The Method of Keeping in God's Love

Jude goes a step beyond the imperative. He gives the command "keep yourselves in the love of God" (v. 21). His command is "sandwiched" between three phrases that show his readers how they can keep themselves in the love of God. Each phrase begins with a Greek participle. Jude is saying, "By building up yourselves, by praying, and by looking, keep yourselves in the love of God." Alford describes the importance of these activities, saying that they are to be "the habit of the life"[5] for the Christian. So the believer commits himself to the lifelong act of keeping himself in God's love and accomplishes it by developing these daily habits. We keep ourselves in God's love by time in the Word of God (v. 20), by consistent prayer (v. 20), and by anticipating Christ's return (v. 21).

"Your Most Holy Faith"

Our first life habit to develop is regularly spending time in God's Word. By the statement "your most holy faith," Jude means more than the believer's faith in God. He began his epistle by speaking of "the faith which was once delivered to the saints" (v. 3). That phrase refers to God's revealed Word. It is logical that he now commands them to keep themselves in God's love by building themselves up on that "most holy faith" (v. 20). Paul described the power of God's Word to the Ephesian elders when he said, "And now, brethren, I commend you to God, and to the word of His grace, which is able to build you up, and to give you an inheritance among all them which are sanctified" (Acts 20:32). The Word of God builds believers and reveals God's love to them.

---

[5]Ibid.

Scripture also exhorts God's people to maintain what Alford called "a habit of life." Job testified, "I have esteemed the words of his mouth more than my necessary food" (Job 23:12). If we need physical food daily, much more do we need to daily feed our souls on the spiritual food of God's Word. Concerning God's Word, Moses urged Joshua to "meditate therein day and night" (Josh. 1:8). David describes the godly man, saying, "But his delight is in the law of the Lord, and in his law doth he meditate day and night" (Psa. 1:2). Jeremiah added, "Thy words were found, and I did eat them: and thy word was unto me the joy and rejoicing of mine heart: for I am called by thy name, O Lord God of hosts" (Jer. 15:16). The Christian cannot find any substitute for the consistent, habitual, and daily practice of spending personal time in God's Word.

a three-times-a-day practice of prayer (Psa. 55:17). Daniel also regularly met the Lord three times daily (Dan. 6:10). Through the basics of time in God's Word and prayer, Christians keep themselves in the love of God.

"Looking for the Mercy of Our Lord Jesus Christ"

We should have no question about Jude's meaning at this point. Alford calls this mercy "that which He will shew at His coming."[8] Our third life habit that keeps us in God's love is expecting Christ's return. We will not develop a prophetic system in this book, but suffice it to say that the New Testament promises Christ's return (John 14:3; I Thess. 4:13-17) and teaches that it could occur at any time (I John 2:28). The apostle John believed in the imminent return of Christ and prayed for it (Rev. 22:20). We do not know when Christ will return, but we are to live every day as if it would be that grand and glorious day.

The Simplicity of Keeping in God's Love

We should note that the Holy Spirit, speaking through Jude, gives us a basic formula for keeping ourselves in this important love relationship with our God. This formula simply involves a disciplined habit of meditating in God's Word, meeting the Lord in prayer, and daily expecting the return of Christ. Preachers and teachers have for years emphasized these basic building blocks of the Christian life. The Bible teaches us that these simple steps are the key to a successful, intimate walk with God.

To illustrate this, we need to remember that many pursuits of life are built on basic principles. When I served Thompson Road Baptist Church in Indianapolis as pastor, we had the renowned gospel pianist Rudy Atwood come for a day of ministry. He wanted to arrive at the church early on Sun-

---

[8]Ibid.

day morning. He went to the piano to practice and asked me to leave the auditorium. I went into my office and left the door open, thinking that I would be blessed by his wonderful gospel music. For about thirty minutes, he played nothing but chromatic scales! He went up the piano keyboard in half steps and back down again. He would then raise the key a half pitch and repeat the process. When he finished that exercise, he played half of a familiar hymn and then stopped. With that preparation he played special numbers, accompanied the congregation and the choir, and played a great concert in the evening service. I was so amazed by his "warming up" routine that I asked him about it. He explained that the basic foundations of music are critical to proper performance. He also told me that he spent proportionately little time practicing his gospel music and more time practicing classical music, which he never performed. He again stressed the importance of the basics of music, saying that if he kept up on the classics, the gospel music, which blessed so many thousands of people in a fifty-year ministry, would "take care of itself," as he put it.

The Christian life is no different. Jude instructs us, "keep yourselves in the love of God" (v. 21). He tells us these basic, essential habits of life are God's appointed way for us to obey this command.

A Crucial Exhortation

Jude's imperative is far more important to this generation of Fundamentalist Christians than we realize. Its urgency, coming near the end of the New Testament era, indicates this fact. Keeping ourselves in God's love is not negotiable. Rather, it is imperative for Christians. Scripture tells us why Jude's command is so important.

First, we must remember that the Christian life is a walk with God. The Bible's teaching of salvation shows that truth.

Genesis 3 teaches that sin separates men from God. When Adam and Eve sinned, they hid from God when He came for what was apparently a regular, appointed time of fellowship. Sin ruptured that communion. The purpose for which God sent Christ to this earth was to reconcile men to God (II Cor. 5:14-21; I Pet. 3:18). Believers are to use their great privilege of fellowship with God (Heb. 10:19-22). Salvation is not mental assent to a doctrinal formula, but a personal relationship with God, entered into when men repent of their sin and trust Christ as their Savior (Acts 20:21). God saves sinners so that they can fellowship with Him. Believers enjoy a permanent relationship with their Lord but must diligently maintain their fellowship with Him. Jude describes the basics of the Christian life.

Second, the greatest commandment God has given men is "And thou shalt love the Lord thy God with all thine heart, and with all thy soul, and with all thy might" (Deut. 6:5; Matt. 22:37; Mark 12:30; Luke 10:27). When Jude charges us to keep ourselves in God's love, he is stressing our first responsibility to God.

Third, we must realize that as Christians our love for God is a response to His love for us. John forthrightly states, "We love him, because he first loved us" (I John 4:19). If we are to love our God as we should, we must first be continually conscious of His love for us. The issue of a Christian's love for God is vitally important in Scripture.

From this proper love relationship of a believer with his God flow the issues of obedience to God, separation from sin, a right attitude toward material possessions, and faithfulness in Christian service.

Fourth, militant, separatist Christians apparently need this exhortation in order to maintain a biblical balance in their lives and ministries. Jude's imperative comes near the conclusion of his warnings concerning the enemies of the faith. God gives a similar warning in a similar passage of Scripture. In His letter to the Ephesian church (Rev. 2:1-7), Jesus commends the church for its militance. These people had labored faithfully and sacrificially in Christ's service (Rev. 2:1, 3). Further, the church had no tolerance for evil people and had discovered and exposed false apostles (Rev. 2:2). Yet the Lord Jesus rebuked them: "Nevertheless I have somewhat against thee, because thou hast left thy first love" (Rev. 2:4). That love was not lost but forsaken. Jude's command to "keep yourselves in the love of God" (v. 21) takes on added importance when we see that believers can get so wrapped up in the legitimate work of God, so involved in sacrificial service, and so committed to biblical militancy that they forsake the love of God. The work of God, sacrifice, and militancy are right. However, they must be seasoned with a fervent love for God. This generation of Fundamentalists needs to be diligent to obey this first-century command.

Conclusion

We live in momentous days and are called to contend for God's revealed truth. We are also called upon to expose and warn against ungodly men who subvert the faith. Yet in so doing we must never forsake our walk with God. Our focus must be on staying in His love. The Word of God reveals God's love. The Holy Spirit will aid us in prayer as we fellowship with our God. We should live in the light of the promise that He will receive us to Himself and that His coming could occur at any time. Developing these life habits will keep us in God's love and obedient to our God.

THE FUNDAMENTALISTS' FERVENCY

The harvest white, with reapers few is
   wasting
And many souls will die and never know
The love of Christ, the joy of sins forgiven.
Oh let us weep and love and pray and go!

Today we reap, or miss our golden harvest!
Today is given us lost souls to win.
Oh then to save some dear ones from the
   burning.
Today we'll go to bring some sinner in.[1]

And of some have compassion, making a difference: *And others save with fear, pulling them out of the fire;* hating even the garment spotted by the flesh (Jude 22-23) [emphasis mine].

Jude describes several characteristics of first-century New Testament Christianity in his letter. He asserts that Christianity rests on the foundation of a revealed Bible. He explains that Christians must earnestly contend for their faith and oppose the interlopers who turn God's grace into lasciviousness and deny the lordship of Jesus Christ. He instructs these same Christians to keep themselves in God's love. Believers obey Jude's command when they develop certain habits of life—namely, building themselves up with Scripture, praying in the Holy Spirit, and looking for Christ's return. These daily disciplines keep the believer in an intimate relationship with his God. Christianity must not only be a theological formulation, but a living fellowship of the believer with the Creator.

---

[1]John R. Rice, "So Little Time" in *Soul-Stirring Songs & Hymns* (Murfreesboro, TN: Sword of the Lord Publishers, 1972), p. 409. Used by permission.

Jude now turns to his last characteristic of New Testament Christianity. He urges believers to look outward to lost people who are affected by these who have encroached upon the true faith. Some doubt the truth that all lost people are under God's judgment, and many are greatly corrupted by sin's depravity. Believers must reach out compassionately and attempt to save them from hell with the message of Christ and His gospel.

A Mark of Fundamentalism

Evangelism was clearly a trait of first-century Christianity. But is it a mark of the twentieth-century movement we call Fundamentalism? Are we reading something into the historic movement to say that Fundamentalism emphasized spreading the gospel to lost men in all the world? We can safely declare that evangelism was (and is) a mark of the Fundamentalist movement.

The Fundamentals

In 1909 Bible believers published a multi-volume defense of Biblical orthodoxy called *The Fundamentals*. This set (now combined into four volumes) continues in print today. Volume 3 contains eight articles on the subject of missions and evangelism, evenly divided between evangelism at home and abroad.[2] Although the analysts of the movement do not necessarily stress evangelism as a hallmark of the movement, it is clear that Fundamentalists understood worldwide evangelism to be a major distinctive of their developing movement.

---

[2]R. A. Torrey et al, eds., *The Fundamentals: A Testimony to the Truth* (1917; reprint, Grand Rapids: Baker Book House, 1970), III:5-6.

Fundamentalist Leaders

The ministries of early Fundamentalist leaders also attest to the emphasis Fundamentalists placed on worldwide evangelism. A. T. Pierson, R. A. Torrey, L. W. Munhall, J. Wilbur Chapman, Bob Jones Sr., W. B. Riley, J. Frank Norris, and T. T. Shields were all fervent evangelists in their own right. Several of them also had a profound impact on the work of missions around the world. A later generation of Fundamentalist leaders, including B. Myron Cedarholm, R. V. Clearwaters, Bob Jones Jr., Monroe Parker, and John R. Rice, carried on ministries of evangelism, church planting, and church building in America and also aggressively advanced the cause of worldwide evangelism.

Pierson was a missionary statesman in his own right. Bob Jones Jr. was an evangelist and founded the Gospel Fellowship Association's mission agency. He actively promoted the work of world evangelism and visited missionaries all over the world. Monroe Parker was gifted as an evangelist. While president of Pillsbury Baptist Bible College, he spearheaded the founding of Baptist World Mission, later serving as its general director for twenty-five years. B. Myron Cedarholm served eighteen years as general director of the Conservative Baptist Association of America. During his tenure, he personally planted many churches, inspired hundreds of others in the church-planting work, and promoted the cause of world missions. Later, as president of Maranatha Baptist Bible College, Cedarholm challenged scores of students to go to various mission fields around the world. Without question, evangelism stands as a defining mark of Fundamentalism.

Jude's Approach

Certain New Testament passages teach clearly the doctrinal nature of the gospel. Romans 3:21-31; 10:4-12; II Corinthians 5:17-21; Galatians 1:6-12; Ephesians 1:4-14; and

Hebrews 2:9-18 are representative passages that teach the theological nature of the gospel. Jude deals with the gospel differently. Certainly the gospel is part of "the faith which was once delivered to the saints" (v. 3). Jude's references to "the common salvation" (v. 3) and "the grace of our God" (v. 4) serve as references to the gospel. But Jude's emphasis appears to be on the believer as the proclaimer of the gospel rather than on the substantive nature of the gospel itself. This does not minimize the truth of the gospel, but rather stresses the heart of the soul-winner. We need God to touch the hearts of present-day Fundamentalists and to give us a clear understanding of lost people's peril as we proclaim the grace of God to salvation. Jude goes on to describe the attitudes that must characterize Fundamentalist soul-winners.

Compassion Because Some Doubt

The first attitude for which Jude calls is compassion. He commands us to show mercy toward those who doubt. God's desire is for "all men to be saved, and to come unto the knowledge of the truth" (I Tim. 2:4). Scripture further teaches that He "is longsuffering to us-ward, not willing that any should perish, but that all should come to repentance" (II Pet. 3:9). God is patient, willing to save men, and He wants men to trust Christ and avoid eternal judgment. The soul-winner will reflect God's compassionate attitude toward the lost. Lovik clearly understands the Holy Spirit's emphasis when he says,

> Jude desires that the believers not be anxious to bring the eternal judgment of God upon them. Jude warns the believers not to strive so earnestly for the faith that they fail to present the faith to those who are in the greatest need. The believers should continually reflect their inward rela-

tionship to God by showing a spiritual concern for the ungodly who have brought division into the church.[3]

The word for "making a difference" speaks of those who have fallen under the influence of false teachers and thus waver.[4] The New Testament uses the expression "making a difference" several times "with reference to weakness in the faith."[5] The false teacher's victims are not necessarily openly opposed to the gospel, but are "beset with inner doubts and questions which must be compassionately dealt with."[6] They wrestle with doubts concerning the truth of Christianity.[7] Thomas Manton calls them "the ignorant and seduced."[8] These people are "at odds with themselves."[9] Jude instructs Christians to show compassion, or mercy, upon these waverers who need to come to Christ. Blum goes on to say, "They must be dealt with patiently and mercifully by showing them Christian love."[10]

A few years ago two young men knocked on the door of a family that attends the same church I attend in Huntsville, Alabama. They were proselytizing for the cult of which they were members. The lady of the house spent some time giving them the gospel. They agreed to return for another session. Dr. Greg McLaughlin, who is my pastor, asked me to meet with them. We spent an afternoon discussing their teachings and the contrasting truths of the gospel. We confronted them

---

[3]Gordon H. Lovik, *"These Men" in Your Church* (Minneapolis: Central C. B. Seminary, n.d.), p. 45.

[4]D. Edmond Hiebert, *Second Peter and Jude* (Greenville, SC: Unusual Publications, 1989), p. 288.

[5]Ibid., p. 289.

[6]Ibid.

[7]Edwin A. Blum, "Jude," in Frank E. Gaebelein, ed., *The Expositor's Bible Commentary* (Grand Rapids: Zondervan Publishing House, 1981), 12:395.

[8]Thomas Manton, *An Exposition of Jude* (Wilmington, DE: Sovereign Grace Publishers, 1972), p. 357.

[9]Blum, p. 395.

[10]Ibid.

with the biblical plan of salvation in clear and certain terms. Never in my ministry have I been more aware of being in a spiritual battle with the powers of darkness than I was on that day. Neither of the young men trusted Christ, but we parted on friendly terms. They promised to return with one of their superiors for another meeting. They later canceled that meeting, having been forbidden by their leaders to meet in that home again. A year or two later one of the young men called the lady in whose home we had met. He informed her that he had doubted the claims of his cult and had left it. We do not know if he has been saved, but compassionate confrontation with the truth certainly produced the Holy Spirit's convicting power in his life.

Within the last few months, one of our Baptist World Mission Board members, Dr. Ralph Wingate, accompanied me to Albania. After we both preached in an evangelistic service, a college student stood publicly to confess that she had trusted Christ and been saved that evening. We learned that she had been studying to become a member of a cult. Doubters can be saved when God's people lovingly give them the gospel of Christ.

These doubters are not necessarily the false teachers themselves. These who waver are likely the ones who have fallen under the influence of the apostates. The false teachers themselves may be beyond the reach of the gospel. Paul does seem to hold out hope for the repentance of some who cause catastrophe to the faith of others (II Tim. 2:18, 24-26). Jude appears to regard the apostates of whom he writes as beyond recovery (vv. 4, 8, 13, 15).

Remember that in dealing with the rich young ruler, Jesus loved him in his unbelief (Mark 10:21). He also told the parable of the good Samaritan who had compassion on the wounded traveler. Christ is the fulfillment of the Samaritan parable. He is God's demonstration of love for sinners (Rom.

5:6-8). Constrained by Christ's love (II Cor. 5:14, 15), we must show mercy to those who need Christ. Our compassion for lost people should send us to them with the gospel of Jesus Christ.

Conviction That All Are Damned

Jude commends a second heart attitude to Christians as they view the lost. He says, "And others save with fear, pulling them out of the fire" (v. 23). Compassion and a sense of urgency must characterize our work with the lost.

Instruments of Salvation

Scripture instructs us to "save with fear" those who are lost. We must remember that God devised the plan of salvation for men before He created the world (II Tim. 1:9). The Bible declares that He only is the Savior (I Tim. 4:10). Jesus alone has the power to save men from sin (Heb. 7:25), and He is the only way to God the Father (John 14:6). He clearly taught us that eternal life is a right relationship with God the Father, which is received only through God the Son (John 17:2, 3). Men cannot save men. Yet here Jude uses unusual language in commanding his readers to "save" those who are lost. The biblical facts show that Christians must "endeavour to be instruments of their salvation."[11] Soul-winners become "God's instruments"[12] of salvation when they give the gospel of God's grace to those who are in danger of eternal judgment.

The Urgency of Salvation

Jude uses strong language to describe the work of evangelism. Believers pull sinners out of the fire when they lead them

---

[11]Manton, p. 359.
[12]Blum, p. 395.

to Christ. This imagery, used also in the Old Testament, describes the danger of impending judgment and the peril in which the lost find themselves. Amos, reminding the northern kingdom of Israel of God's previous deliverance and coming judgment, says that they were "as a firebrand plucked out of the burning" (Amos 4:11). The Lord described Joshua the high priest as "a brand plucked out of the fire" (Zech. 3:2). It seems clear that Jude describes the work of evangelism as urgent because men are in danger of divine judgment.

This imagery also portrays the reality of eternal judgment in hell. "The picture is of a person slipping into the eternal fire but rescued from error by the grace and truth of God."[13] The Bible repeatedly teaches that hell, the place of God's eternal judgment, burns with fire. In the Old Testament, Moses described the fire of hell (Deut. 32:22), as did Isaiah (Isa. 33:14; 66:24). In the Gospels, Jesus repeatedly warned of hell fire (Matt. 13:41, 42; 25:41; Mark 9:43-48; Luke 16:19-31). Paul wrote of eternal, fiery judgment in II Thessalonians 1:8, and John spoke of the lake of fire in Revelation 20:10-15 and 21:8.

Believers need to realize that the doctrine of hell and eternal punishment is under attack today. The shocking reality is that whereas formerly Bible-denying theologians and cultists denied the truth of eternal judgment, now many who claim the label "evangelical" question the Bible's teaching on this subject. Some advocate the annihilation of the lost or a second chance for the lost to be saved in eternity. Others question whether the fire in hell is literal, as the Bible indicates.[14] In antithesis to such academic surmising, the Bible clearly teaches that hell is a place of permanent, eternal judg-

---

[13]Ibid., p. 395.

[14]For a good discussion of the debate on eternal judgment see Larry Dixon, *The Other Side of the Good News* (Wheaton, IL: BridgePoint, 1992). Dixon also treats well the biblical teaching on the subject of everlasting punishment.

ment (Rev. 20:10-15), that it is a place of fiery judgment (Mark 9:43-48; Rev. 20:10, 15; 21:8), and that the lost will be punished there forever (Rev. 21:8). Lost people really are under the condemnation of hell, and they will stand without excuse before God (Rom. 1:20). We who claim the heritage of New Testament Christianity must proclaim the "whole counsel of God" (Acts 20:27), including the revealed truth about hell. When that truth grips the Christian's heart, he gladly will go to lost people at home and in all the world with the biblical message of salvation.

Caution to Avoid Sin's Defilement

Finally, Jude teaches Christians to "save" the lost "with fear," "hating even the garment spotted by the flesh" (v. 23). The Christian fears lest he be contaminated by the defilement of sin.[15] A. T. Robertson calls this "fear of the contagion of sin while we are rescuing them."[16] While loving sinners and showing mercy to them, and while moved by the conviction that lost men are under condemnation, Christian soul-winners must exercise caution not to let sin's filth affect them. Believers must love the sinner but hate his sin.

Some years ago the AIDS epidemic forced its way into the world's consciousness. One of the first high-profile AIDS sufferers was the actor Rock Hudson. In his final months, he went to France for treatment. He was desperately seeking medical help that could save or lengthen his life. The attempt proved futile. Medical experts knew much less about the disease then than they now understand. Reports at the time indicated that while in France, Hudson was kept in complete

[15]R.C.H. Lenski, *The Interpretation of I and II Epistles of Peter, the Three Epistles of John, and the Epistle of Jude* (Minneapolis: Augsburg Publishing House, 1966), p. 648.
[16]A. T. Robertson, *Word Pictures in the New Testament* (Grand Rapids: Baker Book House, 1932), p. 195.

isolation. Food was passed into his room on disposable tableware. His bedding and clothing were burned. After some time, he returned to the United States and soon after died. Even today medical personnel use "universal precautions" to guard against accidental transmission of the virus. Caregivers do all they can to help those who are sick, but simultaneously they diligently seek to avoid infection with disease.

Scripture describes sin as a deadly disease (Isa. 1:5, 6; Rom. 3:10-18). Christians must exercise caution to keep themselves pure while they compassionately seek the salvation of those outside God's grace.

The Scope of Evangelism

Jude says nothing about the scope of evangelism in his little epistle. We must understand that this book is an integral part of the whole New Testament and that its truth will fit consistently with the teaching on evangelism revealed in the rest of the New Testament. Individual local churches must devote themselves to consistent, systematic evangelistic outreach as part of their total ministries in their local areas. All Christians must also give themselves to consistent witness and work with lost sinners in their daily lives. As they live separated lives and seek to avoid the defilement of sin, their testimonies will square with and give validity to the gospel message they verbally give to the unsaved.

The New Testament teaches that local churches and Christians must carry the gospel to all the world. Jesus gave His apostles the Great Commission (Matt. 28:18-20; Mark 16:15; Luke 24:46-49; John 20:21-23; Acts 1:8). The early churches fulfilled the Great Commission as Christ left it with them when He ascended to heaven (Acts 1:8; 5:28; 8:4; 9:31; 13:1-3). The early churches became missionary churches (Col. 1:5, 6; I Thess. 1:7, 8). In addition to the apostles, New

Testament Christians who are not named gave themselves to missionary work (III John 5-8).

Fundamentalist history is interwoven with the history of missions. We cannot review a history of the modern missions movement here, but it is sufficient to say that Fundamentalism has always been an intensely evangelistic and missionary movement. A. T. Pierson, who wrote articles in *The Fundamentals* collection, was a missionary statesman. Several missionary agencies developed as Fundamentalists sought service agencies that would consistently stand for the Word of God against invading modernism.

Dr. Monroe Parker's long ministry as an evangelist is well known. He stood during his entire ministry for Baptist Fundamentalism and against modernism and New Evangelicalism. From 1958 to 1965 he served Pillsbury Baptist Bible College as its president. Battling the compromise within the Conservative Baptist movement, in early 1961 he called for the formation of a new mission agency. Baptist World Mission became a reality on September 15 of that year. Parker served Baptist World Mission as general director from 1969 until his passing in 1994.

Conclusion

New Testament Christianity zealously seeks the salvation of lost people. This zealous commitment to evangelism also characterizes Fundamentalism. Evangelistic fervor is a logical part of biblical Christianity. Fundamentalists accept the Bible as God's revelation. Thus they accept all that the Bible teaches, including what it teaches about man's sinfulness, his need of a Savior, God's grace revealed in Christ, and man's eternal doom without Christ. These truths send Fundamentalists to lost people the world over with the gospel of Jesus Christ.

155

New Testament Christianity exhibits a biblical spirit in the work of evangelism. Christians should love the lost, and they should preach, witness, and work with the conviction that hell is real and that people without Christ face its eternal punishment. In this work they become God's agents of salvation in bringing men to Christ. They must also exercise caution to avoid defilement by the sin from which they seek to save men.

Dr. Monroe Parker modeled the heart of a biblical Fundamentalist as a soul-winner, evangelist, and missionary statesman. While serving as president of Pillsbury, Dr. Parker wrote,

> From jungles far away,
> From town and hamlet small,
> Come cries of souls sin-bound,
> And doomed to endless woe.
> All your hearts with love aflame,
> Arise and to them go![17]

New Testament Christianity produces a fervent effort to win lost sinners to Christ. Our risen Lord commissioned that work for "Jerusalem, and in all Judea, and in Samaria, and unto the uttermost part of the earth" (Acts 1:8). Preceding generations of Fundamentalists have sacrificially and fervently worked to fulfill that commission. The present generation of Fundamentalists must give themselves to the biblical task with biblical fervency.

---

[17]Monroe Parker, Pillsbury Baptist Bible College hymn. Used by permission.

CONCLUSION

Jude has described the nature of New Testament Christianity for us. *First,* New Testament Christianity stands on the foundation of God's Word. Scripture is not a human book but a completed revelation from God. It is "the faith which was once delivered unto the saints" (v. 3). *Second,* New Testament Christians "earnestly contend" for that faith (v. 3). The Christian life itself is a contest, as is the fight for the faith. Militance is an essential part of any Christianity that claims biblical authenticity. *Third,* New Testament Christians will stand against and expose the foes of the faith (v. 4). Jude boldly exposed those who perverted the grace of God and denied the Lord Jesus Christ. Christians today must firmly oppose current apostates who deny the faith. *Fourth,* New Testament Christians also maintain a clear, single focus—to keep themselves in God's love (vv. 20, 21). Using the disciplined habits of time in Scripture and prayer and looking for the return of Christ, they nurture a relationship with God in which they are constantly aware of His love for them. *Fifth,* New Testament Christians fervently work for the salvation of lost men (Jude 22, 23). They show a compassion for the lost, and they work out of a conviction that the unsaved are condemned to hell. All the while they exercise caution to avoid the defilement of sin.

Striking Parallels

We have not studied the history of Fundamentalism, but we have looked at analyses of the movement by a wide range of observers. From the liberals to the self-confessed Fundamentalists, all have noted that Fundamentalism is first an affirmation of the supernatural character of a Word revealed from God and recorded for men by the inspiration of God's

Holy Spirit. Historians and theologians universally identify the militant spirit of Fundamentalism as it stands against the enemies of the faith. The Fundamentalist movement, from its inception, displayed a zealous passion for evangelism, both at home and around the world. The parallels between New Testament Christianity as Jude described it and Fundamentalism as it has developed in the nineteenth and twentieth centuries are striking. We conclude that William Ward Ayer was correct when he asserted, "Fundamentalism is apostolic."[1] Fundamentalism is apostolic Christianity revived. Even liberals admit this fact. Earlier in this study I resisted citing a well-known quotation from Kirsopp Lake because his quotation is so widely cited and commonly used. Lake admits the thesis for which we have argued in this book, saying,

> It is a mistake, often made by educated persons who happen to have but little knowledge of historical theology, to suppose that Fundamentalism is a new and strange form of thought. It is nothing of the kind: it is . . . the survival of a theology which was once universally held by all Christians. The Fundamentalist may be wrong; I think that he is. But it is we who have departed from the tradition, not he, and I am sorry for the fate of anyone who tries to argue with a Fundamentalist on the basis of authority. *The Bible and the corpus theologicum of the Church is [sic] on the Fundamentalist side* [emphasis mine].[2]

Scripture confirms for us what twentieth-century observers, whether Fundamentalist or liberal, have declared.

---

[1]William Ward Ayer, speech to the National Association of Evangelicals, April 1956, quoted in Louis Gasper, *The Fundamentalist Movement, 1930-1956* (1963; reprint, Grand Rapids: Baker Book House, 1981), pp. 2-3.

[2]Kirsopp Lake, *The Religion of Yesterday and To-morrow* (Boston: Houghton Mifflin, 1925), pp. 61-62. Cited in David O. Beale, *In Pursuit of Purity: American Fundamentalism Since 1850* (Greenville, SC: Unusual Publications, 1986), p. 4.

Encouragement

The realization that Fundamentalism bears the marks of New Testament Christianity should offer great encouragement to present-day Fundamentalists. When we affirm the supernatural character of Scripture, when we militantly contend for the faith, when we expose the enemies of the faith, when we emphasize the importance of an intimate walk with God, and when we actively seek the salvation of lost men around the world, *we practice New Testament Christianity!* We can rejoice to follow the trail of men like Hengstenberg, Godet, and Spurgeon, who stood for the Word of God against the invasions of Rationalism and Liberalism in Europe. We can proudly identify with leaders like W. B. Riley, R. T. Ketcham, Bob Jones Sr., Bob Jones Jr., R. V. Clearwaters, B. Myron Cedarholm, and Monroe Parker, who stood for biblical Christianity and against the ravages of modernism. Gratefully, we honor the memory of these and others who perpetuated this biblical faith and passed it on to our generation. Our security and confidence, however, are not based on our godly heritage, but on the realization that our faith is firmly grounded on the Word of God! This realization should produce great boldness in our ranks.

Self-identity

Jude's fivefold description of New Testament Christianity convincingly identifies Fundamentalism. Amazingly, some present-day Fundamentalists have agonized in trying to understand what Fundamentalism is. Several of them have concentrated on the eccentricities and shortcomings of Fundamentalist leaders, thus attempting to justify abandoning or modifying the movement.[3] Sumner's book is an argument

---

[3]One of the first such attempts was Robert L. Sumner, *Fundamentalist Foibles* (Ingleside, TX: Biblical Evangelism Press, 1987). The cover of the book states, "A

that separatism was not part of early Fundamentalism. He argues against separatism, stating, "Separation was never an issue in early Fundamentalism!"[4] Others criticize the supposed inconsistencies, failures, and harsh spirit of certain Fundamentalist leaders. Personally, I am weary of those who identify themselves as Fundamentalists, yet seem to expend all their energy in criticizing and denigrating brethren within the movement. Several who have focused on the negative elements in the movement have forsaken it and its biblical roots for New Evangelicalism and open compromise in ecumenical endeavors. Men are imperfect, even after their salvation. Examination of any Fundamentalist leader's life will reveal imperfections and inconsistencies that reflect the fallen Adamic nature. We ought not excuse such failures, nor should we emulate them. Biblical self-examination is always profitable (I Cor. 11:28). We should abhor our sin and failures and constantly seek Christlikeness through the Holy Spirit (II Cor. 3:18). The Bible teaches us to grow in grace (II Pet. 3:18). Preachers are mandated to serve with a gentle spirit (II Tim. 2:24-26). In addition, we must constructively evaluate and continuously seek to improve our churches and ministries. We should rigorously evaluate our own movement.

Having said all that, we must also remind the negativist critics of Fundamentalism that they also reflect such imperfections and inconsistencies! God uses men, though they are imperfect. Whatever imperfections are obvious, we must also firmly state that they do not negate the rightness of the biblical position we embrace. We should not discard a biblically correct position because we dislike the actions of certain individuals.

Look Back at our 'Roots'! Who Was Considered 'A Fundamentalist' in the Early Days? Have We 'Changed the Rules' in Our Day?"
[4]Ibid., p. 22.

Early Fundamentalists, when they attacked liberals, assailed doctrinal abuses. I watched Fundamentalist leaders like Monroe Parker, Myron Cedarholm, Richard Clearwaters, and Ernest Pickering stand against New Evangelicalism. They fought the flawed and unscriptural philosophies of compromise and ecumenism. I grieve to see present-day disgruntled descendants of these giants look back with contempt on the courageous heroes of that generation and attack them!

In the South we have a beautiful flowering bush called the crepe myrtle. A couple of years ago my wife instructed me to plant one behind our house, and I dutifully complied. Through all the hot weather of summer it produces gorgeous red blooms. Early in the spring of each year, Judy prunes back that bush. Following the advice of horticulturalists, she annually cuts the crepe myrtle back to one-third its size. The first time she cut that bush back, I thought she had killed it! However, she knew what she was doing, and the thorough pruning resulted in vigorous spring growth and another summer of full, rich bloom.

We may need to closely examine and severely prune the "bush" of our Fundamentalist movement. If we are committed to excellence, we will always look for ways to improve our walk with God, ministries, and methods. Pruning will invigorate our ministries.

Pruning, however, does not attack the plant at the roots to dig it up or destroy its life. It seeks to produce vigorous growth. Yet that very destructive tendency appears within the ranks of Fundamentalism. Many men were saved, called to ministry, and trained because of the sacrificial leadership and selfless work of Fundamentalist preachers. Yet now they seem to concentrate solely on the flaws in the men and the movement that nurtured them. Without any gratitude, they criticize those who paid a price to give them the spiritual heritage they now demean. Such action borders on treason.

161

We all can find flaws to avoid in men, even in those who are our heroes. Let us feel free to objectively examine ourselves and our movement. Let us use our influence to improve Fundamentalism's testimony in this evil day. Let us prune the plant and cut back the dead wood. But let us remember that the plant of Fundamentalism grows in a rich, fertile, biblical soil. Let us never desert the ranks for compromise!

When Dr. Monroe Parker served as Pillsbury College's president, he had a statement in the student handbook and also quoted it as he felt necessary. It said, "Constructive suggestions are always welcome, but destructive criticism will never be tolerated!" We should approach Fundamentalism with the same attitude. Our movement is biblically defined. Let us plant this generation of ministry and testimony firmly on that biblical foundation. We must determine to commit that heritage to faithful men who follow us, just as we received it from many witnesses. Let us deal objectively and kindly with our shortcomings. But let us not become so discouraged with or focused on the imperfections that we forsake the biblical parameters Jude marks out for us. Some today are doing that. All the negative energy could be better used in positive action to improve the movement. Our movement is biblically defined, and we need no insecure and introspective musings about who we are.

A Road Map for the Future

Understanding our biblical frame of reference will enable us to meet the future. Fundamentalism has had to face changing attacks from Satan. The Fundamentalists of the 1920s had to stand against open liberalism. Later Fundamentalists had to stand against liberalism and the moderation of fellow Bible believers who compromised with it, creating New Evangelicalism. These men withstood the ecumenical evangelism of

Billy Graham. Today a similar ecumenism faces this generation of Fundamentalists as the Promise Keepers movement. No one would ever have dreamed that evangelicals would make a mad dash for Roman Catholicism such as we see today in the Evangelicals and Catholics Together. Instead of the philosophy of Schleiermacher and his German Rationalism, this generation must stand against the fatalism of postmodern thinking and its denial of absolute truth. The issues have changed, and we can rest assured that Satan will produce new attacks if Jesus tarries. We have the confidence that our faith rests on an absolute, inspired revelation from God. That Word from God will give us the foundation on which to stand and the truth with which to fight as we face new issues in succeeding generations. May God enable us to "earnestly contend for the faith which was once delivered unto the saints" (Jude 3) in every situation we face. We enjoy a heritage preserved for us by heroes of days past. May God graciously grant that we preserve that heritage and pass it on to our children and grandchildren.

SELECTED BIBLIOGRAPHY

Books and Commentaries

Alford, Henry. *The Greek New Testament*. Cambridge: Deighton, Bell and Company, 1862.

Armstrong, John H., ed. *The Coming Evangelical Crisis*. Chicago: Moody Press, 1996.

Ayer, William Ward. Speech to the National Association of Evangelicals, April 1956. Quoted in Louis Gasper, *The Fundamentalist Movement, 1930-1956*. 1963. Reprint, Grand Rapids: Baker Book House, 1981.

Barnes, Albert. *Notes on the New Testament: James, Peter, John, and Jude*. 1848. Reprint, Grand Rapids: Baker Book House, 1979.

Barr, James. *Fundamentalism*. Philadelphia: The Westminster Press, 1977.

Beale, David O. *In Pursuit of Purity: American Fundamentalism Since 1850*. Greenville, SC: Unusual Publications, 1986.

Blum, Edwin A. "Jude." *The Expositor's Bible Commentary*. Edited by Frank E. Gaebelein. Grand Rapids: Zondervan Publishing House, 1981.

Bush, L. Russ and Tom J. Nettles. *Baptists and the Bible*. Chicago: Moody Press, 1980.

Chemnitz, Martin. *Examination of the Council of Trent*. Vol. I. Translated by Fred Kramer. St. Louis: Concordia Publishing House, 1978, p. 37. Quoted in John E. Milheim, ed., *Let Rome Speak for Herself*. Schaumburg, IL: Regular Baptist Press, 1982.

Colson, Charles. *The Body*. Dallas: Word Publishing, 1992.

Copeland, Kenneth. *Believer's Voice of Victory.* February 1987. Quoted in John F. MacArthur Jr., *Charismatic Chaos.* Grand Rapids: Zondervan Publishing House, 1992.

Deere, Jack. *Surprised By the Voice of God: How God Speaks Today Through Prophecies, Dreams, and Visions.* Grand Rapids: Zondervan Publishing House, 1996.

Dixon, Larry. *The Other Side of the Good News.* Wheaton, IL: BridgePoint, 1992.

Erickson, Millard J. *Christian Theology.* Grand Rapids: Baker Book House, 1985.

Falwell, Jerry, ed. *The Fundamentalist Phenomenon.* Garden City, NY: Doubleday & Company, Inc., 1981.

Feinberg, Charles L. *The Minor Prophets.* Chicago: Moody Press, 1980.

Gill, John. *Body of Divinity.* 1769-70. Reprint, Atlanta: Turner Lassetter, 1965.

Gray, James M. "The Inspiration of the Bible—Definition, Extent and Proof." In *The Fundamentals.* Edited by R. A. Torrey. Grand Rapids: Kregel Classics, 1958.

Grudem, Wayne. *Systematic Theology: An Introduction to Biblical Doctrine.* Grand Rapids: Zondervan Publishing House, 1994.

Henry, Carl F. H. *The Uneasy Conscience of Modern Fundamentalism.* Grand Rapids: Wm. B. Eerdmans Publishing Company, 1947.

_____. *God, Revelation and Authority.* Waco, TX: Word Publishing, 1976.

Hiebert, D. Edmond. *Second Peter and Jude: An Expositional Commentary.* Greenville, SC: Unusual Publications, 1989.

Hills, Edward F. *The King James Version Defended.* Des Moines: The Christian Research Press, 1984.

Hoad, Jack. *The Baptist*. London: Grace Publications Trust, 1986.

Hodge, Charles. *Systematic Theology*. 1871. Reprint, Grand Rapids: Wm. B. Eerdmans Publishing Company, 1993.

Holthaus, Stephan. *Fundamentalismus in Deutschland, Der Kampf um die Bibel im Protestantismus des 19. und 20. Jahrhunderts*. Bonn: Verlag für Kultur und Wissenschaft, Dr. Thomas Schirrmacher, 1993.

Horton, Michael, ed. *The Agony of Deceit*. Chicago: Moody Press, 1990.

_____. *Made in America*. Grand Rapids: Baker Book House, 1991.

Kyle, Joseph. "The Word of God—The Foundation of the Fundamentals." In *God Hath Spoken: Twenty-five Addresses Delivered at the World Conference of Christian Fundamentals*. Philadelphia: Bible Conference Committee, 1919.

Lenski, R.C.H. *The Interpretation of St. Paul's Epistles to the Colossians, to the Thessalonians, to Timothy, to Titus, and to Philemon*. Minneapolis: Augsburg Publishing House, 1946.

_____. *The Interpretation of the Epistle to the Hebrews and the Epistle of James*. Minneapolis: Augsburg Publishing House, 1966.

_____. *I and II Epistles of Peter, the Three Epistles of John, and the Epistle of Jude*. Minneapolis: Augsburg Publishing House, 1966.

Lindsell, Harold. *The Battle for the Bible*. Grand Rapids: Zondervan Publishing House, 1976.

Lovik, Gordon. *These Men in Your Church: An Exegesis of the Book of Jude*. Minneapolis: Central C. B. Seminary, n.d.

MacArthur, John F. Jr. *Charismatic Chaos*. Grand Rapids: Zondervan Publishing House, 1992.

Manton, Thomas. *An Exposition of Jude*. Wilmington, DE: Sovereign Grace Publishers, 1972.

Marsden, George. *Fundamentalism and American Culture*. Oxford: Oxford University Press, 1980.

_____. *Reforming Fundamentalism: Fuller Seminary and the New Evangelicalism*. Grand Rapids: Wm. B. Eerdmans Publishing Company, 1987.

Masters, Peter. *The Healing Epidemic*. London: The Wakeman Trust, 1988.

Moritz, Fred. *Be Ye Holy: The Call to Christian Separation*. Greenville, SC: Bob Jones University Press, 1994.

Morris, Leon. "Hebrews." In *The Expositor's Bible Commentary*. Edited by Frank E. Gaebelein. Grand Rapids: Zondervan Publishing House, 1981.

Osborne, Grant R. *The Hermeneutical Spiral*. Downers Grove, IL: InterVarsity Press, 1991.

Pache, René. *The Inspiration and Authority of Scripture*. Chicago: Moody Press, 1969.

Packer, J. I. *"Fundamentalism" and the Word of God*. Grand Rapids: Wm. B. Eerdmans Publishing Company, 1962.

Parker, Monroe. *More Desirable Than Gold*. Decatur, AL: self-published, 1963.

Patterson, Paige. In John L. Dagg. *Manual of Theology and Church Order*. Harrisonburg, VA, 1982, flyleaf.

Pickering, Ernest D. *The Tragedy of Compromise*. Greenville, SC: Bob Jones University Press, 1994.

Pickering, Wilbur. *The Identity of the New Testament Text*. Nashville: Thomas Nelson Publishers, 1977.

Pierson, A. T. *Seed Thoughts for Public Speakers.* New York: Funk and Wagnalls Co., 1900.

Rawlinson, George. "Isaiah." In *The Pulpit Commentary.* Edited by H.D.M. Spence and Joseph S. Exell. New York: Funk and Wagnalls Company, 1909.

Riley, William Bell. "What Are the Real Questions Before the Northern Baptist Convention?" *Baptist*, June 18, 1921. Quoted in Grant Wacker, *Augustus H. Strong and the Dilemma of Historical Consciousness,* Macon, GA: Mercer University Press, 1985.

_____. "Modernism in Baptist Schools." In *Baptist Fundamentals.* Philadelphia: The Judson Press, 1920.

Robertson, A. T. *Word Pictures in the New Testament.* Grand Rapids: Baker Book House, 1932.

Ruckman, Peter S. *The Christian's Handbook of Manuscript Evidence.* Pensacola, FL: Pensacola Bible Press, 1970.

Ryrie, Charles C. *Basic Theology.* Wheaton, IL: Victor Books, 1986.

Sandeen, Ernest R. *The Roots of Fundamentalism.* Grand Rapids: Baker Book House, 1970.

Sidwell, Mark. *The Dividing Line.* Greenville, SC: Bob Jones University Press, 1998.

Strombeck, J. F. *Disciplined by Grace: Studies in Christian Conduct.* Moline, IL: Strombeck Foundation, 1975.

Strong, Augustus Hopkins. *Systematic Theology.* Valley Forge, PA: The Judson Press, 1907.

Sumner, Robert L. *Fundamentalist Foibles.* Ingleside, TX: Biblical Evangelism Press, 1987.

Tenney, Merrill C. "The Gospel of John." In *The Expositor's Bible Commentary.* Edited by Frank E. Gaebelein. Grand Rapids: Zondervan Publishing House, 1981.

Torrey, R. A., et al., eds. *The Fundamentals: A Testimony to the Truth.* 1917. Reprint, Grand Rapids: Baker Book House, 1970.

Unger, Merrill F. *Introductory Guide to the Old Testament.* Grand Rapids: Zondervan Publishing House, 1956.

Vincent, M. R. *Word Studies in the New Testament.* 1887. Reprint, Grand Rapids: Wm. B. Eerdmans Publishing Company, 1989.

Vine, W. E., Merrill F. Unger, and William White Jr., eds. *Vine's Expository Dictionary of Biblical Words.* Nashville: Thomas Nelson Publishers, 1985.

Wallace, Daniel B. *Greek Grammar Beyond the Basics.* Grand Rapids: Zondervan Publishing House, 1996.

_____. "Inspiration, Preservation, and New Testament Textual Criticism." In *New Testament Essays.* Edited by Gary T. Meadors. Winona Lake, IN: BMH Books, 1991.

Warfield, B. B. *The Inspiration and Authority of the Bible.* Philadelphia: The Presbyterian and Reformed Publishing Company, 1948.

Wells, David F. *No Place for Truth.* Grand Rapids: Wm. B. Eerdmans Publishing Company, 1993.

White, James R. *The King James Only Controversy.* Minneapolis: Bethany House Publishers, 1995.

Williams, James B., ed. *From the Mind of God to the Mind of Man: A Layman's Guide to How We Got Our Bible.* Greenville, SC: Ambassador-Emerald International, 1999.

Reference Works

Arndt, William F. and F. Wilbur Gingrich. *A Greek-English Lexicon of the New Testament.* Chicago: The University of Chicago Press, 1957.

The Articles of Faith of the Church of Jesus Christ of Latter-day Saints. Salt Lake City: Corporation of the President of The Church of Jesus Christ of Latter-day Saints, 1988.

Bauernfeind, Otto. "ἀσέλγεια." In *Theological Dictionary of the New Testament.* Edited by Gerhard Kittel. Reprint, Grand Rapids: Wm. B. Eerdmans Publishing Company, 1975.

The Book of Mormon. Salt Lake City: Corporation of the President of The Church of Jesus Christ of Latter-day Saints, 1981.

Bultmann, R. "μένω." In *Theological Dictionary of the New Testament.* Edited by Gerhard Kittel. Reprint, Grand Rapids: Wm. B. Eerdmans Publishing Co., 1975.

Fawcett, John. "How Precious Is the Book Divine." In *Hymns of the Christian Life.* Camp Hill, PA: Christian Publications, Inc., 1976.

Lake, Kirsopp. *The Religion of Yesterday and To-morrow.* Boston: Houghton Mifflin, 1925. Cited in David O. Beale, *In Pursuit of Purity: American Fundamentalism Since 1850.* Greenville, SC: Unusual Publications, 1986.

Leith, John H., ed. *Creeds of the Churches.* Garden City, NY: Doubleday and Company, Inc., 1963.

Lumpkin, William L. *Baptist Confessions of Faith.* Philadelphia: The Judson Press, 1959.

Rengstorf, Karl Heinrich. "δεσπότης." In *Theological Dictionary of the New Testament.* Edited by Gerhard Kittel. Grand Rapids: Wm. B. Eerdmans Publishing Company, 1964.

Rice, John R. "So Little Time." In *Soul-Stirring Songs &
Hymns*. Edited by John R. Rice. Murfreesboro, TN: Sword
of the Lord Publishers, 1972.

Rippon's Selections, 1787. "How Firm a Foundation." In
Hymns of the Christian Life. Camp Hill, PA: Christian
Publications, Inc., 1976.

Schlier, Heinrich. "βεβαιόω." In *Theological Dictionary of the
New Testament*. Edited by Gerhard Kittel. Grand Rapids:
Wm. B. Eerdmans Publishing Co., 1964.

Seventh-day Adventists Believe . . . Washington, DC: Ministerial Association, General Conference of Seventh-day
Adventists, 1988.

Stauffer, Ethelbert. "ἀγών, ἀγωνίζομαι and Compounds." In
Theological Dictionary of the New Testament. Edited by
Gerhard Kittel. Grand Rapids: Wm. B. Eerdmans Publish-
ing Company, 1964.

Thayer, Joseph Henry. *Greek-English Lexicon of the New Testament*. Grand Rapids: Zondervan Publishing House, 1962
edition.

Vine, W. E. *An Expository Dictionary of New Testament Words*.
Westwood, NJ: Fleming H. Revell Company, 1966 edition.

Wigram, George V. *The Englishman's Greek Concordance of the
New Testament*, 9th edition. London: Samuel Bagster and
Sons, 1903.

Journals and Magazines

Combs, William W. "Errors in the King James Version?" *Detroit Baptist Seminary Journal*, fall 1999, p. 160.

Dobson, Edward. "I Am Proud to Be a Fundamentalist." *Fundamentalist Journal*, June 1985, p. 12.

Doran, David M. "Defense of Militancy." *The Sentinel* (Detroit Baptist Theological Seminary), spring 1995, pp. 1-2.

Farnell, F. David. "Fallible New Testament Prophecy/ Prophets? A Critique of Wayne Grudem's Hypothesis." *The Master's Seminary Journal*, n.d., p. 161.

_____. "The Current Debate about New Testament Prophecy." *Bibliotheca Sacra*, July-September 1992, p. 280.

_____. "The Gift of Prophecy in the Old and New Testaments." *Bibliotheca Sacra*, October-December 1992, pp. 39-405.

Grounds, Vernon. "The Nature of Evangelicalism." *Eternity*, February 1956, p. 13.

Grudem, Wayne A. "Still Prophesy." Quoted in F. David Farnell, "Fallible New Testament Prophecy/Prophets? A Critique of Wayne Grudem's Hypothesis," *The Master's Seminary Journal*, n.d, p. 161.

_____. *The Gift of Prophecy in the New Testament and Today*. Westchester, IL: Crossway Books, 1988, pp. 14-15. Quoted in F. David Farnell, "The Current Debate about New Testament Prophecy," *Bibliotheca Sacra*, July-September 1992, p. 280.

Harris, Richard A. "A Plea for Christian Statesmanship." *The Challenge*, December 1997, p. 1.

Jones, Bob Jr. "As I See It." *Preach the Word*, January-March 1998, p. 12.

McCune, Rolland D. "The Self-Identity of Fundamentalism." *Detroit Baptist Seminary Journal*, spring 1996, pp. 9-34.

Pettegrew, Larry D. "Will the Real Fundamentalist Please Stand Up?" *Central Testimony*, fall 1982, pp. 1-2.

Singleton, James E. "Tensions Between Older and Younger Fundamentalists!" *Whetstone*, May 1998, p. 4.

Tulga, Chester E. "The Fundamentalism of Yesterday, the Evangelicalism of Today, and the Fundamentalism of Tomorrow." *Testimonies*, May 1998, p. 7.

_____. "What Baptists Believe About Soul Liberty." *The Baptist Challenge*, October 1997, p. 21.

Vanhetloo, Warren. "Indications of Verbal Inspiration." *Calvary Baptist Theological Journal*, spring 1989, p. 63.

Wood, Charles. *Pastoral Epistle* (South Bend, IN: personal publication), June 1998, p. 5.

Bibles

Morris, Henry M., ed. *The Defender's Study Bible*. Grand Rapids: World Publishing, Inc., 1995.

"The Translators to the Reader." In *The Holy Bible, a Facsimile in a reduced size of the Authorized Version published in the year 1611*. Oxford: Oxford University Press, 1911.

Miscellaneous

Burggraff, David L. "What Will Keep Us from Becoming New, New Evangelicals?" Calvary Baptist Theological Seminary. Lecture notes.

_____. Calvary Baptist Theological Seminary. Lecture notes.

Cummins, David L. Letter to Fred Moritz, April 13, 1998.

Delnay, Robert. *Distinctive Marks of Fundamentalism.* Clearwater Christian College. Lecture notes.

Dogmatic Constitution on Divine Revelation DEI VERBUM Solemnly Promulgated By His Holiness Pope Paul VI November 18, 1965. Rome: Vatican Web Site, http://www.vatican.va.

Know Your Roots: Evangelicalism Yesterday, Today, and Tomorrow. Two hours. 2100 Productions, 1991. Videocassette.

Lippincott, Lester L. III. "A Study of 'That Which Is Perfect' in First Corinthians 13:10." Th.M. thesis, Detroit Baptist Theological Seminary, 1990.

McCune, Rolland D. "A Biblical Study of Tongues and Miracles." Central Baptist Theological Seminary, n.d.

_____. "Systematic Theology I." Detroit Baptist Theological Seminary. Class syllabus.

McLachlan, Douglas R. "Fundamentalism: What's in a Name?" Central Baptist Theological Seminary, 1998. Lecture notes.

Ockenga, Harold John. Press release. Boston: The Park Street Church, December 8, 1957.

Parker, Monroe. Pillsbury Baptist Bible College Hymn.

Pickering, Ernest D. "Systematic Theology." Central Baptist Theological Seminary, 1963. Lecture notes.

_____. Field Representative, Baptist World Mission. Telephone interview by author, September 30, 1999, Decatur, AL.

Wicker, Christine. "Even R-Rated Films Suggest Redeeming Messages to Believers With Eyes to See." *The Dallas Morning News,* June 6, 1998, p. 1G.

Zichterman, Joe. "A Passion for Thee." In *We're Singing*, 6th ed. Taylors, SC: THE WILDS Christian Association, Inc., 1997.

SCRIPTURAL INDEX

TOPICAL INDEX

Vine, W. E., 29, 83, 139, 140

Wacker, Grant, 15
Wallace, Daniel B., 81-87
Warfield, B. B., 37, 39, 45, 70-
  71
Watchman Examiner, 10
Wells, David, 123-24, 126
Westminster Confession, 78-79
White, Ellen G., 41
Williams, James B., 92
Wood, Charles, 3
World Conference on Christian
  Fundamentals, 67
World Congress of Fundamen-
  talists, 23
worldliness, 17

Zichterman, Joe, 131